EXORCISM!

EXORCISM!

Peter Underwood

ROBERT HALE · LONDON

© Peter Underwood 1990
First published in Great Britain 1990

Robert Hale Limited
Clerkenwell House
Clerkenwell Green
London EC1R 0HT

British Library Cataloguing in Publication Data
Underwood, Peter, 1923–
Exorcism!
1. Exorcism
I. title
133.4'27

ISBN 0–7090–4017–2

Photoset in Palatino by
Derek Doyle & Associates, Mold, Clwyd.
Printed in Great Britain by
St Edmundsbury Press Ltd, Bury St Edmunds, Suffolk.
Bound by WBC Bookbinders Limited.

Contents

For
my grandson
Joe Derby
in gratitude for
all his interest
and help

Illustrations

PICTURE CREDITS

Chris Yates: 1; Ghost Club: 2, 4, 5, 10, 11, 12, 15, 17, 25, 27; Vandyk: 3; Peter Underwood: 6, 9, 13, 14, 16, 21, 24, 28; National Trust for Scotland: 7; British Tourist Authority: 8; Downing, *Daily Express*: 18; Chris Underwood: 19; Sean Manchester: 20; Bassano and Vandyk: 22; F.W. Holiday: 23; German National Museum, Nuremberg: 29; British Museum: 30.

Acknowledgements

Julio Caro Baroja for telling me about possession and exorcism in Spain.

Kenneth C. Breen, Head of History, St Mary's College, Strawberry Hill, Twickenham, for details of the Horace Walpole sales.

The British Film Institute for confirming dates and facts.

Commander A.G.W. Bellars OBE for information about the Loch Ness exorcism.

Mrs Honor Cobb for telling me about her father, Sir C. Aubrey Smith.

Marie Devine, Librarian, The Lewis Walpole Library, a department of Yale University, for her generous help in respect of the Cellini bell.

The Germanic National Museum, Nuremberg for supplying me with a photograph of a painting in their possession and for permission to reproduce it.

Renée Haynes for putting me right about Charles Dickens' adventure in Genoa.

Ernest Hecht for allowing me to use an extract from Dr Ainslie Meares' book, *Strange Places and Simple Truths* (Souvenir Press, 1969)

Ann and Michael Joy for their friendly co-operation.

Stewart Lamont for talking to me about ghosts, haunted houses and exorcism.

Los Angeles Times for their write-up of the court case when the Devil was named as co-defendant.

Sean Manchester for allowing me to recount his adventures in hunting the Highgate vampire and for the use of his photograph.

Jean Marshall for information about Dent authors.

Sheila Merritt for cuttings from American newspapers and other information.

Arthur Peters for obscure information about San Zeno.

Edwin Pouncey for information and photographs of Montague Summers.

Hugh Tate, Department of Medieval and Later Antiquities, British Museum for providing me with the full history of the Cellini bell.

Dr Devandra P. Varma, Professor of English, Dalhousie University, Halifax, Nova Scotia, for imparting to me some of his enthusiastic knowledge of vampires.

Dr Clive Wainwright, Assistant Keeper, Department of Furniture and Interior Design, Victoria and Albert Museum, for putting me on the track of the Cellini bell.

Canon Dominic Walker OGS Rural Dean of Brighton, for his interest and help.

Gordon Wellesley for talking to me about Jewish and other religious exorcisms.

And last, but not least, I am immeasurably indebted to my wife for her interest, encouragement and practical help.

Introduction – And a Look at Biblical, Chinese and Italian Exorcisms

Throughout history the rite of exorcism in one form or another has been used not only by every religion but also by pagans and the irreligious for the purpose of driving out evil spirits and demons that are thought to possess afflicted human beings.

Exorcism, as we shall see, has also been used at Loch Ness, at accident 'black spots', to 'cure' a killer lion, to restore good luck to a fishing trawler and even to combat the apparently mysterious forces at work in the area known as the Bermuda Triangle – and in a score of other strange circumstances.

A succinct definition of exorcism would be the use of the name of a deity to expel evil spirits from places and people.

Early examples of exorcism are to be found in the Scriptures, for it was a not uncommon profession among the Jews.

Matthew 12: 27 and 28 read, 'And if I by Beelzebub cast out devils, by whom do your children cast *them* out? ... But if I cast out devils by the Spirit of God, then the kingdom of God is come unto you', and again, Mark 9: 38 and 39: 'And John answered him, saying, Master, we saw one casting out devils in thy name, and he followeth not us: and we forbad him because he followeth not us. But Jesus said, Forbid him not: for there is no man which shall do a miracle in my name, that can lightly speak evil of me.' In fact, exorcists themselves are referred to in Acts 19: 13: 'Then certain of the vagabond Jews, exorcists, took upon them to call over them which had evil spirits the name of the Lord Jesus, saying, We adjure you by Jesus ...'

Long before Christianity there were such acts as cleansing ceremonies and the bottling of evil spirits by such ancient races as the Chinese and the Egyptians. Today the great bulk of the Chinese race, according to Colonel Valentine Rodolphe

Buckhardt DSO, OBE, shares the cynicism and indifference expressed in the views of the Roman proconsul, according to Francis Bacon: 'What is truth, said jesting Pilate, and would not stay for an answer.'

Colonel Buckhardt first visited China just before the First World War and, apart from the war, he spent many years travelling through the country in such varied capacities as interpreter (first class) and military attaché to the British Embassy. Always interested in Chinese creeds and customs, he made a special study of this subject during his remaining years and there are or ever have been few, if any, better informed on the subject.

We met and talked about Chinese ways and customs on several occasions at Ghost Club meetings, and I remember he said that, while ancestor-worship is the hard core of all Chinese belief, creating a morality that implied that an unworthy action was an offence against one's ancestors and that a blameless life ennobled them, had become part of two leading organized religions, Taoism and Buddhism. To gain acceptance, both religions have had to accept or tolerate the primeval Chinese beliefs. Earth gods were added and easily accepted but still Taoism in its pure form made little progress in the land of its birth for its followers, for, instead of attempting to infuse harmony into practical life, it sought freedom for its followers from the material.

In seeking to achieve their ambition to escape the body and become free and powerful spirits, followers were required to lead a hermit-like existence and abandon family ties – which mean more in China than anywhere else on earth – and isolation for the community at large. Since Taoism had little hope of commending itself to a society so gregarious as the Celestial Empire, it was transferred into a popular religion by Chang Tao-ling (b.AD34), 'the First Master of Heaven', an investor of magical spells who also introduced charms and talismans to ward off evil spirits from man and beast.

This 'Master of Heaven' was the supreme exorcist and was credited with possessing a cellar of evil spirits, bottled up in jars and corked with his seal. Forty years ago Buckhardt told me that Tao-ling was still a power in the land and that his cabalistic antidotes for averting misfortune were published annually in a calendar. He founded a school of exorcists and introduced faith-healing into medicine. Such a new form of insurance, against just about any form of calamity, had a great popular appeal, and the religion spread like wildfire; not least because there was emphasis on exorcism and the care of the souls of the departed.

In certain cases and especially when a member of the sect was ill, these departed souls would be conjured from the vasty deep, usually in the hope of contacting the spirit responsible for the malady but sometimes in the hope that prayers and entreaties would avail a cure. Then it might be necessary to exorcize the subject and banish the dead souls back to the regions of the departed.

Buddhism includes doctrines of reincarnation and purgatory. The Chinese found it difficult, if not impossible, to accept the idea of eternal punishment after death, and the idea of hell had to be considerably modified before it could be accepted! Spirits of the departed were awarded three holidays a year, when they were free to revisit the earth, a whole month being granted at the time of the Seventh Moon and shorter recesses at the spring and autumn equinoxes.

'Ancestor-worship' imposed the necessity of caring for souls in the afterlife, and the hells were carefully organized, on the lines of the imperial administration, with magistrates to enforce justice, warders and tormentors. All of these ghosts were credited with the grasping attributes of their earthly counterparts, and so the dead had to be supplied with money to ameliorate their treatment. Thus special services and dispensations of food, money and clothing were arranged for the benefit of ghosts deprived of the ordinary care that would be theirs, due to the extinction of the family responsible for their maintenance, to prevent their becoming any kind of menace to the community of the living during their return holidays to earth.

Exorcism was always an essential part of the consecration of a Chinese shrine. Furniture could be donated; craftsmen would give their services free, constructing incense-burners and a carved scarlet and gold screen to frame the images of the Deity, with the its decorations of tree peonies and two lucky bats. Images of the deities were said to be unconscious of their surroundings until their eyes had been opened with the touch of blood drawn from the comb of a cock.

The Chinese share the universal belief in ghosts and have adopted the ancient Roman methods of propitiating them: as long as the spirits are fed, they will do no harm to mortals, hence the wide-spread custom of providing food offerings for the hungry ghosts, especially during the Seventh Moon, when they are released from Hell. Spirits of the departed, believe the Chinese, can right injustice or take revenge for injuries suffered during their earthly existence. There are vampires too and mischievous poltergeists, as well as the spirits of those who have met an unnatural death – the latter are greatly feared, as their only means of redemption is to lure a living soul to destruction as a substitute for their own.

Ghosts, say the Chinese, are essentially nocturnal and fade with the coming of the dawn. If they should be surprised by daylight, they will liquidize into a pool of blood. Consequently they have the greatest aversion to the sight of human blood and may be expelled by biting the tip of the middle finger and threatening to rub it on them. The Chinese consider the middle finger to be the master finger and, as the blood is believed to flow to it directly from the heart, its power of conjuration is all the more effective.

In the Peking area, where the dry atmosphere in winter is conductive to the production of electric sparks when friction is applied to fur or hair, the local Chinese have an original method of exorcizing or dispelling ghosts. Spirits, they believe, are scared by illumination and so can be prevailed upon to depart by a strenuous rubbing of the scalp!

Other forms of exorcism in China include lethal firecrackers, candles, incense and fresh eggs that have to be broken. In one such invocation the exorcist also arms himself with offerings of paper clothing, a square of yellow paper, an earthenware teapot and a representation of the Five Demons thought to be at the root of the trouble.

After the candles and incense have been lit on an altar, the name of the client would be communicated to the divinity while at the same time the exorcist waved the yellow paper in front of the images of the Earth God. The crackers were then inserted into the teapot, and the strip of paper with the Five Demons was placed on top of them, care being taken that they were head downwards, so that their skulls received the full impact of the blast. Offerings to the deity were then burned and the blazing mass was passed to and fro over the incense before being carried out to a brazier. The officiant then took the eggs and, removing one, broke it into a bowl so that the shell was shattered. More paper and talismans were lighted at the altar candles, and then the fuse of the crackers was ignited and the onlookers drew back in preparation for the explosion. This soon took place, pieces of the teapot flying in all directions.

Before the smoke cleared, the exorcist returned and examined the debris for any trace of the Five Demons. Nothing being found, it was regarded as a good omen, and the name of the afflicted was written on a piece of paper and burned to reveal his or her identity as the one responsible for the sacrifices; more incense was lighted, a prayer intoned, more paper offerings were waved over the incense and, accompanied by an invocation, a second egg was smashed into the bowl; the service of exorcism concluded with the burning of the remainder of the paper.

In cases where devils were thought to be causing disease or ill-fortune, they were dispelled by taking a garment belonging to the patient or person who was suffering bad luck, and peanuts were knotted into the garment; these were thought to act as prisons for the offending spirits. Next the exorcist furnished himself with candles, incense, clothing belonging to the unfortunate 'victim' and money, consisting of gold squares printed in the centre of white sheets of paper. These would all be carried to the seashore, where a sand altar would be erected on which the incense and the candles would be lit. The mother of the afflicted person, or the nearest relative, would kneel, facing the sea, and make her intercession for the removal of the disease or bad fortune. Lighting a bonfire of the sacrifices, she would take the victim's clothing and, still praying, pass it several times with a circular motion over the bonfire. To dispel the demons, now believed to be confined or tricked into the centre of the paper with the gold squares, this would be folded into a paper boat and set adrift, to carry away the evil. The garment that had been knotted would then be unknotted and the peanuts removed. One would be thrown away to the left, one to the right and a third over the shoulder behind the petitioner. This was believed to dispose of the land-based demons who had been scattered to the four winds of heaven.

Colonel Buckhardt told me that, in the late thirties, after

witnessing one such expulsion of devils causing disease, he made a number of enquiries and discovered that the mother had first consulted 'a wise woman' who had 'diagnosed' the cause of her offspring's affliction, a wasting disease. The wise woman asked for no fee other than the customary honorarium of a few cents, 'lucky money'. She carefully examined the child's hand and declared that the child was frightened of the water; it was for this reason that the exorcism had been carried out at the sea shore.

If a child had a narrow escape from being run down by a car, Buckhardt learned, and suffering shock affecting the appetite, for example, a similar service would be held in front of a parked car. In such a case, part of a bucket of water would be thrown over the car, and the residue taken home and used to bathe the patient; afterwards the water would be thrown away and with it the devils afflicting the child, it was thought.

Usually, to get rid of devils, rice moistened with water would be employed, but in the case witnessed by Buckhardt it was felt that water might not be entirely beneficial, and peanuts were prescribed instead. Such home remedies are cheaper than calling in a doctor, and in many cases they achieve equally satisfactory results. The idea of 'a hair of the dog that bit them' is believed in quite literally, and should an indisposition be attributed to a local and identified dog, a tuft of the animal's coat would be procured and tied with a card or ribbon around the patient's neck.

Children the world over fear the dark, and in old China steps were taken to deal with any demons who might be hovering near, ready to pounce during the dark hours of night. The cubbyholes where the children slept were fumigated by burning charms and sacred paper, and if all else failed, the explosion of crackers completed and finalized the exorcism.

Yet another form of exorcizing or placating Chinese mischievous ghosts was detailed to me by Colonel Buckhardt. There is or was a Festival of the Hungry Ghosts that ranked high in the order of popularity, only surpassed in fact by the New Year celebrations. For centuries the country clung to the old custom in memory of its nameless dead, the ghosts of those who had died honourable deaths.

These spirits haunt the places where their bodies perished, and they hunger for food as, their graves being unknown, they are bereft of family care and worship at the ancestral altar. They are forever seeking a substitute to regularize their position but they will never molest those who feed them. Hence the Feeding of the Hungry Ghosts by all sections of the population is or was universally popular, especially during the Seventh Moon when the dead are released and able to return to earth. The Festival of the Hungry Ghosts dates, I was told, from the earliest days of Buddhism.

The history of ghosts has been likened to a mystery play, a ritual drama in which characters play their parts, take their bows and disappear. First there is man with his hopes and dreams, next a ghost – a man without a body. A man must be honoured in his grave or he will return; a man who is wronged will return; a man who does wrong will return – and in each case when he returns he will be a fearful creature, embodying all the terrors of the dark world from which he has returned.

Mankind has devoted a considerable amount of his time to this ghost or ghoul or devil or angel that he feels he may one day become. He has sought to comfort himself with the idea of a haven in the beyond where his sins will be forgiven and he will not need to return, or he has rejected the idea of a dead person's consciously returning and comforted himself with the idea that ghosts are shadows of past events, with no actuality, no substance, but rather belong to 'such stuff as dreams are made on'.

Exorcists in the ancient world laid down rules for the control of ghosts, whose behaviour they had studied with great care. First they would track down the ghost to its hiding-place – perhaps the place where it had died or was buried or had lived; then they would discover its likes and dislikes, and having done so they set about destroying the poor ghost. That they never succeeded is probably due to the fact that each generation had to learn afresh the ritual and ceremony of effective exorcism, while the ghost, by all accounts and in some mysterious way, seemed and still seems always a step ahead of its hunters, some of whom have embraced the cult of spiritualism and sought to meet the ghost on its own ground.

Into this difficult realm step the religious exorcists, and since both Roman Catholic and Anglican Churches have long regarded spiritualism as wrong, because it traffics with the spirits of the dead, neither has entered upon the challenge with much enthusiasm. This, it may be said, in spite of the fact that spiritualists are avowed Christians and are usually only too willing to collaborate with either of the orthodox religions in conducting services of exorcism. So each goes his way alone: the Roman Catholic with his view of confession and forgiveness, the Anglican with his all-powerful prayers, and the spiritualist with his co-operation to the extent that he is prepared for the ghost to borrow his body and manifest through him.

Of course there are some more enlightened individuals who have experienced ghosts, hauntings, possession and the like and sought to examine and explain them on rational grounds. Such a man was Sir Shane Leslie. 'We are constantly confronted with hauntings where priests have been summoned to lay the ghost ...' he says in his *Ghost Book*. 'If ghost or wandering soul it is, the saying of prayers or Masses is the proper course. In cases of obsession or diabolical intervention the Church has provided Exorcism.' Not that such activities are enthusiastically welcomed by either Church for, as Sir Shane delicately puts it: 'Priests who pay too much attention to ghosts find themselves discouraged in their careers in the manner in which Naval captains who log the sea-serpent in the course of a cruise are disapproved at the Admiralty.'

I remember discussing with a leading Unitarian theologian the idea of evil as a reality and the possibility of actually being possessed by an evil spirit. He told me: 'I find that few people attempt to come to grips with the real problem, which is whether evil has actual objective reality in the world of the spirit. Lewis Spence possessed a wealth of remarkable knowledge and a cautious judgement, and in one of his books he talked about the deliberate and organized worship of evil (Satanism) but such activity may, of course, be no more than the worship of an illusion – a pathological perversion of normal instincts and desires, and to my mind he never commits himself on this vital issue. Personally I believe that evil is something much more real and objective than a mere perversion can ever be. Just as I believe in the objectivity of goodness, exemplified not only in devout human souls but also discarnate spiritual entities and consummated in the being of God, so also do I believe in the perpetuation of evil in discarnate souls in the realm of the spirit.'

I found what he had to say so interesting that I pressed him to continue, asking his views on a 'Prince of Evil'. He replied: 'I should say that this belief of mine in evil does not involve the objective reality of a Prince of Evil – a Satan – corresponding to the reality of God, for evil is ultimately destructive, and those souls that continue to cleave to evil impulses are destined finally to psychical disintegration. From them shall be taken away even that individuality which they have. Goodness integrates, evil disintegrates; goodness edifies whereas evil destroys; hence there can be no everlasting reality for evil. It belongs to temporal reality, not to the nature of the eternal. Goodness alone is eternal, and only those human souls that choose the way of goodness can become truly immortal. Evil souls truly survive death and may, indeed I believe do, continue to influence souls living in this mortal world, but they can have no enduring triumphs. If only we had the faith and the virtue and the strength to regenerate this our present world, I believe we should do much to cleanse and redeem the world of the spirit also. To believe this is to intensify the urgency and the significance of the moral struggle. In this respect liberal religion has been weak and uncertain; evangelical religion is more nearly right where this is concerned, for this world and the next are closely linked in this moral conflict.

'As time passes and life moves on, I find myself getting less interested in formal philosophy (of which I think I have read my share) and more and more interested in mystical and occult literature, for the reason that in the latter there is the hint of knowledge too subtle for our normal understanding to grasp. No doubt much in occultism must be regarded as symbolic rather than as actual knowledge, but that does not invalidate it or lessen its worth, for if the symbol points to some reality which rationalism, with its own restricted technique, cannot apprehend, then it stands for a Truth that is greater than more prosaic processes of thought can attain to. For this reason, I am quite willing to allow speculation to outrun the evidence to a fair extent, especially if it rounds off and fulfils experience which reason cannot explain, and I believe that our psychological development necessitates that we shall trust imagination and creative idealism far beyond the limits of normal perception. We have to trust the finger-posts if we would travel, and we shall never reach the far country if we always keep our eyes on our feet.'

On a somewhat different tack, the Rev. Donald Omand once said to me: 'I think a tremendous harm was done when the Church ceased to preach about the Devil, because therein lies his strength. If nobody believes in his existence he has the power to do anything. That being so, I believe completely in what is written in the New Testament and I believe that Our Lord was the greatest exorcist of all time.'

In the early 1930s, when he was a journalist, Donald Omand interviewed Adolf Hitler three times. Hitler was born in the Austrian frontier town of Braunau, as were Willi and Rudi Schneider, world-famous and thoroughly investigated psychic mediums; perhaps there is something in the air in that part of the world, for Hitler had an almost mediumistic power over people, and at least one person who should know, Albert Speer, once said: 'To be in his presence for any length of time made me tired, exhausted and feeling void.' The war historian Alan Bullock says Hitler always '... retained an uncanny gift of personal magnetism, which defies analysis, but which many who met him have described. Hitler's power to bewitch an audience has been likened to the occult arts of the African medicine-man or the Asiatic shaman; others have compared it to the sensitivity of a medium and the magnetism of a hypnotist.' According to French authors Louis Pauwels and Jacques Bergier, Hitler had the same wet-nurse as Willi Schneider – so perhaps they both imbibed something with the milk; certainly, in their own way, powers that Hitler displayed were just as strange and mysterious as those exhibited by Willi Schneider.

Omand told me he was not really aware of Hitler's hypnotic power or of anything very evil about the man, although of course this was before the little Austrian came to real power. Looking back, Omand recalled that he had had the immediate feeling that Hitler needed help; that he was desperately unhappy, dreadfully lonely, and that it was something like the shell of a man that he was meeting, without any substance; empty, part of his personality missing and devoid of the essence and core of a real man. On other occasions it was something quite different. Omand saw Hitler at one of the famous Nuremberg rallies, where he seemed almost possessed and exuded an hypnotic power that was really frightening. Omand told me that when he first met Hitler he had had little experience of evil, and less knowledge of the power of the human mind.

Had he met Hitler years later, he would have tried to exorcize him, and Omand believed he could have done that; not that it would have stopped the Second World War but it might have stopped Hitler from doing some of the terrible things he did and pursuing some of the evil courses that he did pursue.

Having failed to exorcize Hitler, Donald Omand went on to practise exorcism at a circus; on the ghost hound of Kettleness (perhaps Dracula himself!); at Loch Ness and at a score of other strange locations, as we shall see in Chapter 2. He also blessed animals on an annual basis – a far cry from the ancient Greek revels of Dionysus (Bacchus), in part a festival of the dead: a feast that lasted for three days, one of which was considered to be especially unlucky, for it was then that ghosts were abroad; by way of protection, people used to chew buckthorn.

Other, equally ineffective ways were employed to ward off evil. At a Ghost Club meeting many years ago, Dr Alexander Cannon related such an attempt, the details having been supplied to him by the wife of an ex-consul general. This lady spoke of one Eastern belief that was accepted and taken for granted: if an envious person admired a child or caressed it, that child would either die or some evil would overtake it.

The lady also mentioned something that occurred to her many years before, when she was too young to have had either time or inclination to tackle deep subjects. She said: 'I was in the Italian maremma [marshland], between Tuscany and the Roman states, and this happened during the period of my first marriage with a then powerful magnate in the province. Without any apparent reason I found that I was gradually becoming weak and nervous. My colour, which was normally of a healthy pink hue, faded until it entirely disappeared. I became very thin, so that the fact was remarked upon by all my friends. I had no illness whatever, and was not lacking in any luxury or comfort but I was simply wasting away.

'One day a lady called upon me: I knew her only slightly but she asked me to listen to her and to take her advice – for my own good. "You are gradually dying without any apparent reason," she said. "You are the victim of envy. The women of this citadel and of this province envy you and your position, your beauty and your accomplishments, and also the fact that you are English, whereas an Italian lady has more right to be in your place."

'She said she would help me and suggested we went into my dressing-room, where she closed the door carefully and then prepared a basin of water. Into the water she poured some oil which she had brought with her and she murmured what sounded like prayers and made a number of gesticulating signs. At last she said: "Now you are free from the effects of the evil eye, evil wishing and evil influence. You will see that you will soon be better and become your old self again."

'I should say that I merely tolerated this performance, not really believing it would have any beneficial effect or really taking part in the exorcism, for that is what it was. However, it so happened that my health and general state of being did rapidly improve; and events took a turn for the better; things happened favourably for me and I lived to enjoy peace and happiness there. That lady's exorcism worked.'

Dr Cannon said that he was quite aware that, while there are several possible reactions to such an experience, the only logical explanation in accordance with the evidence was that the lady in question was affected by some unknown force and that this was itself affected and rendered ineffective by a form of exorcism.

Such afflictions are or were assumed by some people to be the result of contact with Satan or as evidence of being possessed by devils. The world of medicine was for centuries intermingled with magic, and mental illness in particular was regarded as due to the direct intervention of the Devil. In asylums it was not unknown for attempts to be made to drive out the devils thought to be occupying the bodies of these unfortunate patients by resorting to violence and maltreatment of the harshest kind; it was commonplace for those judged to be insane to be kept chained in dark dungeons, cruelly flogged and put on public exhibition. There was no real treatment for those unfortunate people who thought they heard voices, who had lost touch with reality and whose perception of the world around them was distorted and unreal; no treatment except exorcism.

Not surprisingly perhaps, this elaborate ritual, especially in early days, was rarely successful. The 'bewitched' person, usually terrified and totally unable to comprehend what was happening, would be stripped naked, shaved of all body hair and anointed from head to feet with an odorous oil which contained ashes of olives and holy water. At the same time prayers were intoned, often in Latin, and then followed the frightful forced drinking of a dense and foul liquid (usually 'herbal' in the widest sense), which usually consisted of the matter's being forced down the throat. Often the exorcist also bled the patient, and on occasions a live chicken would be cut into pieces and applied to the head of the wretched man or woman, who by this time would be out of his or her mind with fright and panic.

Further words from the exorcist would be read with authority, force and fervour, and if any twitch or convulsion was observed in the unfortuante wretch being exorcized, the whole process might be repeated, in addition to sprinkling the room again and again with holy water. Not infrequently such exorcisms were effective in as far as the affected person suffered no more: he or she was often dead from suffocation, choking, exposure, loss of blood or just plain fright.

Lay exorcisms, long ago, were even more involved and ingenious. They would force the patient to drink holy water from upturned church bells (and more than one 'bewitched' person drowned in the process); the patient's head would then be held over a bowl of burning brimstone until the face was black with smoke (and more than one patient was suffocated with smoke in this process); then, suddenly and without any warning, a holy relic would be introduced into the proceedings and not infrequently actually introduced into one of the orifices of the body of the patient. The thumb of a long-dead saint was vigorously thrust into the mouth and almost down the throat of one afflicted person, and when he began to choke and scream, the exorcist remarked complacently, 'Hark how the Devil cannot endure holy things.'

John Bunyan has left a graphic description of one exorcism that he attended, and he refers to a '... devil ... that did have the ale-house keeper and rent and tore him till he died.' Bunyan described the flesh of the patient 'gathered up in a heap ... to the unutterable torture and affliction' of the person being exorcized. Then a man 'who was more than an ordinary doctor' attempted to force out the devil. 'They had the possessed ... and laid him upon his belly upon a form, with his head hanging down over the form's end. Then they bound him down thereto, which done, they set a pan of coals under his mouth and put something therein which made a great smoke; by this means, as it was said, to fetch out the devil. There they kept the man till he

was almost smothered in the smoke, but no devil came out of
him.'

Eric Maple related the story of a devil, expelled from the body
of a victim by exorcism, asking plaintively what was to become
of him, now that he was homeless; to which the exorcist replied,
mockingly, 'Go to the privy.' However he lived to regret such
hasty words, for later, on entering the privy himself, he was
suddenly attacked from the rear by the same devil! It was,
understandably, 'a lesson he never forgot'.

Then there is the contemporary account of Bishop Martin of
Tours (c.316 – c.400) which is also not without humour. As he
was about to enter a house, he caught sight of a demon lurking
in the porch. Indignantly the bishop confronted the demon and
ordered it to depart, but the demon, in panic, disappeared into
the house and there took refuge in the body of the cook, and
when that poor man immediately showed every sign of
madness, the bold bishop, nothing daunted and without
hesitation, thrust two of his fingers down the throat of the cook,
defying the demon to have the power to bite his holy fingers:
the demon took the only other way out and departed, leaving, in
the words of the actual account, 'sad and foul traces behind
him'. The cook, it is reported, immediately recovered his senses.

Such extreme measures of exorcizing demons and devils were
not always adopted of course, and Johan Weyer (1516–88), a
Protestant who denied the existence of sorcery and witchcraft,
nevertheless advocated exorcism as a means of getting rid of
such illusions created by Satan to trap mankind. He, however,
believed in fasting and prayers as the most effective
components of exorcism, and some of his methods and ideas are
still practised by exorcists today.

On the other hand the views of King James VI and I, for
example, who tended to discover the work of the Devil in all
sorts of unexpected places, have not stood the test of time,
which is just as well, for he advocated the use of tobacco as a
fumigant to drive out devils; tobacco was, he said, 'a black and
stinking fume … resembling the horrible stygian smoke of the
pit that is bottomless.' He even believed that jugglers were
agents of the Devil, from whom they obtained their
'inexplicable' skills.

Coming almost up to the present day, the already mentioned
Sir Shane Leslie, a Roman Catholic who believed that Catholics

had a right to investigate the ghostly part of the universe as well
as the worldly, talked to me in 1960 on the subject of exorcism.
'If there is one subject in the New Testament that is crystal clear
and completely practical,' he said, 'it concerns the casting out of
devils.'

'Today these statements carry medical rather than theological
significance. Obsessions and possessions are a constant
accompaniment of civilized life. Only medical skill on the one
hand or a wise "discerner of spirits" on the other can exactly
decide or guess whether the malady is of the mind or of the soul,
proceeding from within or from an external influence. Today
"possession" is used to explain musical prodigies and all
manner of "gifted" people.

'Some cases of possession may only be suffering temptations
to take drink or drugs, their own lives or the lives of others. But
there are cases where the impulse can be connected with an
external site or "spirit". In such cases the Church permits the
dread service of exorcism, but only under the strictest
supervision and after exhaustive and evidential enquiries.

'It is generally held that the bishop of the diocese must give
permission and that the exorcist should be a newly ordained
priest, who presumably has no sin upon his conscience. The
genuine demoniac is believed to have power to retaliate by
revealing a knowledge of the exorcist's past life.

'The Church admitted ghosts in the Middle Ages or she
would not have been so hostile when she suspected a diabolical
origin. In dealing with them she certainly developed her own
technique and used a special service for exorcism which has
continued in the armory of the Church, although seldom used
except in a "hole-and-corner" manner. At the same time, it is
not necessary to suppose that either a demon or an angel, an evil
spirit or a saintly one, is the invariable source of manifestations
or messages from the "other world".'

Still on the subject of exorcism, Sir Shane told me at a later
date: 'For those with little knowledge of such matters, it may be
news to learn that permission for a solemn exorcism is very
rarely granted: in fact, it is not easy to lay hands on the text or
precise procedure of the rite.

'The priest authorized by the bishop has to be specially
selected or approved by him. (Cardinal Moran, when Bishop of
Ossory, sent three priests to investigate two nieces of his own in

Kilkenny, aged fourteen and fifteen, who became disturbed by unexplained noises and strange obsessions: these all ceased after exorcism.) Before performing the rite of exorcism, which involves a Mass to be said in or near the haunted premises, as the priest may choose, the latter is bound to observe an absolute fast for twenty-four hours beforehand, during which period he must be as far as possible in a state of prayer, in accordance with the statement attributed to Our Lord that "This kind goeth not out save by prayer and fasting." The episcopal authority allows the selected priest to perform the rite more than once for the same haunting or possession in the event of the first exorcism's apparently proving ineffective. This was regarded as being in accordance with the apostolic command to go on praying and not to faint. It also indicates the Church's recognition that we know little and are indeed not meant to know much, perhaps, in this world about the affairs of the next. Thus it is not a question of science but of faith. The main part of a service of exorcism consists, after special prayers, of a command in the name of Jesus Christ, to the spirit to betake himself to the place appointed. The language used is powerful in its authority, unlike much of the quiet dignity of the Church's rites.' (Sir Shane Leslie said much the same in his volume which he entitled *Shane Leslie's Ghost Book*.)

And therein may lie one of the secrets of exorcism. Those services of exorcism at which I have been present have been very impressive, especially to the occupants of the house that is regarded as haunted. I believe that, having witnessed such an impressive ceremony, the occupants and people concerned, in many cases, notwithstanding that curious happenings may recur, refuse at first to believe that such is the case. The house has been exorcized, therefore it is no longer haunted. As time passes and strange and inexplicable happenings continue, it is no longer possible to comfort oneself in this way, and it has to be accepted that the exorcism has not altogether succeeded; although it has often had a considerably beneficial effect on the human inhabitants, it has had little or no effect on the supernatural inhabitants of the house. That, at all events, is my personal experience.

Nearly every great discovery first appears to the average mind to be a supernatural manifestation, and in a way that is what it is, for such discoveries are additions to humanity's knowledge of the natural; so it is with exorcism: when it works, the average person regards it as a supernatural manifestation, and when it does not work, it is superstition.

Exorcism does not conform to our known 'laws', but then no 'laws' proposed by scientists should be regarded as true for all time; indeed, it can be argued that, if such 'laws' defy physical laws, the so-called 'laws' were never true.

Why does exorcism only work sometimes? It is a mystery, but then at every step of our life, and indeed throughout the history of mankind, we are confronted with mystery. The sublime intellectual eminence of the ancient Greeks is a mystery; the profound moral conscience of the early Hebrews is likewise a mystery. Sometimes exorcism does seem to work, but more often, in my experience, it has no lasting effect. Why this should be so is often no mystery, but the whole question of the efficacy of exorcism hangs in the balance for most thinking people. But let us look a little closer at exorcism and exorcists.

1   Exorcism: Ancient and Modern

We have taken a brief glimpse at some of those who practised ancient exorcism, and perhaps we should look a little closer at exorcism and primitive man, and the practices and rites used to combat evil spirits, before taking a look, by way of contrast, at some of those who claim to be able to perform exorcisms today.

As Eric Maple says in his *Realm of Ghosts*, 'In the world of the savage the phenomena of life is always interpreted in terms of magic, a system of ideas based upon the illusion that an outward similarity implies a logical connection. Thus it is believed possible to influence the fate of a human being by conducting a ritual involving an image of that person or to ensure success in the chase by engaging in an imitation hunt using a model of the animal that is to be hunted. In the same way ghosts must be eluded, deluded, or exorcized by magical means which are usually the monopoly of a witch doctor. The latter, a kind of rudimentary psychiatrist, deals with the psychic problems of men and women who have not yet learned to distinguish between dreams and reality. In fact many of the ghosts of both primitive and modern man are really waking dreams, often terrible in their intensity.'

'Waking dreams' may be a sort of explanation for the experience that some people attribute to ghosts, but examination of the evidence suggests that this simply cannot be the answer to many such experiences. Where it is possibly the explanation, the impressive incantations of a primitive or modern exorcist might well prove successful.

Before the development of any system of law, man, in his darkness and ignorance and superstition, turned to the supernatural and devised ceremonies by which the judgement of some invisible god-like force might be evoked to demonstrate the guilt or innocence of the accused. Such 'ordeals' are known to have existed from earliest times, and even now traces linger on among primitive races, especially in Africa.

One part of the natural world that has always given rise to legends, superstitions and strange powers is the moon; perhaps because of its magic light and its influence on earthly creatures and aspects such as the tides. So ancient are many of these attributes that their origin is forgotten, but throughout the world's legends there are allusions to this tradition.

To mention only one, the whole of Eastern European folklore has the moon as a beautiful maiden, the little sister of the sun: 'Only the sister of the sun, Stands at the gate of paradise.' Other tales tell of the sun's incestuous passion for his own sister, the moon, so the moon went about only at night, when her brother was not in sight. In other legends the moon is regarded as male, and the 'man in the moon' has a lustful attraction for women. Some tribal communities consider the moon to be a lecherous man who roams the earth seeking, especially on nights of the full moon, young virgins to deflower. He is credited with ravishing every maiden on earth, and the token of his success is the onset of menstruation; some Indian tribes refer to the first menstruation as 'defloration by the moon'. Less fanciful and more logically, occultists have always believed that the moon has an immense power of attraction over our bodies and over the bodies of all living beings, constituted as they are largely of liquid elements and so affected by moon power. Might not the human brain, a mass of semi-liquid pulp, be stirred in some strange way by suction or ejection from the moon? Hence 'moon madness' and the established fact that there occurs a noticeable increase in unusual, eccentric and irrational behaviour among many people during periods of the full moon.

On the other side of the coin, the new moon was hailed as beneficial, and the Romanian Marcu Beza, lecturer at King's College, London University, writing in 1928, tells of his grandmother's often approaching him with a soft whisper: 'Come, dear, the new moon!' She would give into his hands a loaf of bread, a silver coin (symbols of prosperity) and two vessels filled with water. She would make him turn round three times and then look straight at the moon, while she would utter, 'with deep religious solemnity', some rhyme that sought goodness, prosperity, good health and happiness for her grandson.

Such addresses, says Marcu Beza, are not mere poetical fancies, 'roused by the wandering beauty of the moon', nor are they simple forms of sympathetic magic; there enters into them, this explorer of legends suggests, 'a pale, far-off remembrance of religious worship.'

Bathing in the waters of a spring, one would be endowed with healing properties; appeals to the moon, either as a good fairy or as an old protecting goddess, could drive away evil spells or one's personal ills, it was thought. So the moon, from an incestuous sister of the sun and deflowerer of virgins, has become a healing property, used, as it is used – or rather invoked, to this day, by exorcists.

One invocation from Eastern Europe has been used within living memory as a form of cleansing and exorcism, perhaps even of prayer: 'O luminous moon, luminous moon, come and take away the spell and the desolation, and the hatred from the world, and from my house, and from my table, and from my garden, and from my vineyard, and from my craft, and from my trade, and from my purse, and drive it away to wild mountains and forests; and us and our children and those who shall be born unto us hereafter, leave us clean and pure like refined gold and like the sun that shines brilliantly in the skies!'

Advancing a little from really primitive man, we reach biblical times and the indisputable fact that Jesus and His early disciples believed in exorcism and in diabolic possession, a fact that is abundantly proved by passages of the New Testament, at least in the judgement of the majority of New Testament scholars. In Matthew 8: 28–33, for example, we read:

And when he was come to the other side [of Lake Galilee] into the country of the Gergesenes, there met him two possessed with devils, coming out of the tombs, exceeding fierce, so that no man might pass by that way.

And, behold, they cried out, saying, What have we to do with thee, Jesus, thou Son of God? art thou come hither to torment us before the time?

And there was a good way off from them an herd of many swine feeding.

So the devils besought him, saying, If thou cast us out, suffer us to go away into the herd of swine.

And he said unto them, Go. And when they were come out, they went into the herd of swine: and, behold, the whole herd of swine

ran violently down a steep place into the sea, and perished in the
waters.

And they that kept them fled, and went their ways into the city,
and told every thing, and what was befallen to the possessed of the
devils.

Mark 3: 22, states that the scribes remarked of Jesus, 'He hath
Beelzebub and by the prince of the devils casteth he out devils.'
Jesus replied to the accusation by saying, 'How can Satan cast
out Satan? ... And if Satan rise up against himself, and be
divided, he cannot stand, but hath an end.' So the question as to
whether 'Beelzebub' and 'the prince of demons' may or may not
be two separate conceptions is left open, but the reply seems to
show that Jesus assumes the reference to be to Satan, the
supreme head of the kingdom of evil.

This Beelzebub (or Beelzebul) is a significant but shadowy
figure. Together with Azazel, Senjaza, Mastema and Belial, he
seems to be one of the chief evil spirits; in the Talmud he is
regarded as a prince among demons. The name is generally
agreed to mean literally 'lord of flies', which suggests he is able
to send or to remove a plague of flies. He is generally pictured as
being of terrifying aspect, enormous in size, black, bloated,
horned and with bat's wings. The artist Felicien Rops depicts
him with his member erect and with a nude woman swooning
in front of him. Other artists have represented Beelzebub as a
serpent or as a pretty woman; Milton described him as an
imposing king whose face radiates wisdom. At all events, the
mighty devil Beelzebub, once regarded as a principal lieutenant
of Satan himself (but relegated by medieval times to a popular
villain in mystery plays), often figures in the confessions of
sorceresses and has been the subject of specific exorcisms –
although of course such confessions were usually of an
hysterical tone that revealed morbid delirium and exaggerated
wishful thinking.

Research shows clearly that such beliefs continued in full
force in the early Church until the end of the fifth century at
least. To name but a few, we find Justin Martyr (d.c.165)
speaking of Jewish and Christian exorcisms, claiming the latter
to be superior. The reality of exorcism is vividly described in the
Clementine Writings (c.180–200) and by Irenaeus (d. c.202), while
Tertullian (d. c.230) goes as far as to equate the power to exorcize
successfully with the reality of a man's Christianity.

Minucius Felix (d. *c*.250) also graphically describes possession by demons and the reality of exorcism. Cyprian (d. *c*.258) describes possession and exorcisms that took place in the third century, while Cyril of Jerusalem (d. 386) describes the ways in which a demon tortures the possessed man and refers to 'the hours of exorcisms' as forming part of the regular services of the Church, referring presumably to 'baptismal exorcism'.

The power of exorcism was once regarded as a special gift, like the power of prophecy; a fact acknowledged by Chrysostom (d. 407), Jerome (d. 420) and Augustine (d. 430), who speaks of exorcism as the general experience and practice of the Church.

With Jesus extolled as the great exorcist as early as the third century, the Church of Rome had found it necessary to provide itself with a contingent of exorcists: according to the letter from Pope Cornelius (251–2) to Fabius, the Roman Church at that time possessed fifty-two exorcists. Edward Langton, writing in 1934, tells us that the seventh canon of the Fourth Council of Carthage (398) prescribes the rite of ordination for the exorcist, and the same rite was 'still in use in the Roman Church'. 'Many exorcisms,' he goes on to say, 'are related to St Benedict [*c*.480–543], the founder of Western Monasticism.'

These early saints have been referred to as 'doctors of the soul', and in addition to exorcizing 'evil spirits' from seemingly possessed men and women, children too came in for similar attention, and there is an account of a monk, Marcarius of Alexandria, curing a child by simply a 'laying on of hands'. We are told that a protégé of Father Anthony, Paul the Simple, encountered a more stubborn 'spirit' when he confronted a man whose 'possession' caused him to roar like a wild beast and shout curses to all and sundry. Paul addressed the demon-possessed man, saying, 'Father Anthony orders you to go forth from this man,' but the devil, through the afflicted man, continued to curse, if anything more vehemently than before. The would-be exorcist then struck the possessed man, at the same time calling out a deterrent that had proved successful previously: 'Go forth and I will go and tell Christ about it.' But the result this time was less than successful; in fact still more obscene blasphemy streamed from the man's mouth and, in desperation, Paul fell onto his knees and prayed fervently to God, declaring that he would neither eat nor drink until the devil had left the body of this man. Suddenly there was a great

cry from the man, and the words the exorcist had longed to hear
burst from the man's lips: 'I am cast out.' It is said that
something like a dragon was seen to leave the body of the man
and wriggle away.

In those early days the act of exorcism was not confined to
ordained clerics; even the simplest and most ill-mannered of the
faithful sometimes cast out demons by a mere prayer of
conjuration (Mark 16: 17), the effectiveness of such exorcisms
'proving', it was thought, the power of Christ's grace and the
inability of the possessing demons to resist it.

Later, after the institution of an order of exorcists, those
practising the cleansing were not always ordained for the
special office of exorcist, and anyone possessing the necessary
charismatic power was recognized and allowed to practise as an
exorcist; a practice that to some extent survives to this day,
although the order of exorcists no longer exists in the Roman
Church, the power of exorcism having been transferred to
higher orders of the ministry.

It is no exaggeration to say that Tertullian (c160–c.230), one of
the most famous and influential of all the Christian teachers of
the period, was obsessed with the idea of demons and devils,
and he traces the origin of such beings to certain fallen angels.
We learn how it was that, from certain unspecified angels who
fell from grace of their own free will, there sprang a brood of
wicked demons. This information comes from 'sacred books',
probably the apocalyptic volumes, and those written under the
name of Enoch in particular. In his treatises this Christian
apologist argues strongly for the genuineness of the 'Scripture
of Enoch', which he contends was published before the Deluge.
Tertullian speaks of such angels rushing from heaven 'on the
daughters of men' and of earthly women who possessed
husbands who were fallen angels – literally.

The Devil, or Satan, chief of these evil spirits, was made by
God, according to Tertullian; one of the angels who became the
Devil or accuser by false detraction from God. When he was
created, he was good but by choice he became corrupt and was
therefore cast down from heaven. Every spirit, both angel and
demon, says Tertullian, is possessed of wings, and all spirits are
endowed with amazing swiftness. So swift are they that they are
everywhere in a single moment; the whole world is one place to
them. Thus it is easy for them to know and to repeat what takes

place in any corner of the earth. It is this facility that gives them the semblance of divinity. They know things so quickly that they are able to give intimations of the future – such teaching, it should be remembered, dominated the thoughts of men throughout the Middle Ages and continued until a couple of centuries ago; even today some religious bigots point to the exponent of divination as one who is in league with evil spirits.

From their dwellings in the air, near the stars, and from their proximity to the clouds, it was thought that such spirits had means of knowing the preparatory processes going on in those upper regions and were thus able to forecast such activity as rain, which they would already feel. So subtle and tenuous were they that they had access to both the body and the soul of man; often invisible, always intangible, their actions were usually known only by their effects. So one can see how persistent, devious, resolute and intellectually agile the exorcists had to be.

The formidable Tertullian was particularly insistent about the power of Christians to exorcize demons, going as far as to assert that those who cannot cast out demons are not genuine Christians! Exorcism, he tells us, is achieved by uttering the name of Christ and by the recitation of the woes with which demons are threatened at the coming of Christ as Judge, accompanied by the touch and breathing of the exorcist.

Other contemporary writers, such as Minucius Felix (c.160–c.250), give vivid accounts of the popular ideas and beliefs concerning demons. Describing them as 'unclean, wandering spirits', Minucius says they have lost their heavenly energy from being weighed down by earthly passions and disorders; they are 'steeped in vice' and, being lost themselves, seek to destroy others. He agrees with Tertullian that such evil spirits conceal themselves in statues and consecrated images, and from those shelters they 'inspire' soothsayers. To attack mankind, they animate the fibres of their victim's entrails, direct the flight of minds of men and draw them away from heaven. Their rarefied and subtle nature enables them to creep into men's bodies, counterfeit diseases, terrify imagination and rack the limbs. It is evil spirits that are responsible for madmen who run about the streets, raging, ranting and whirling around in a foolish dance. It is evil spirits who poison the minds of men with jealousy, cruelty, loss of virility and, conversely, insatiable sexual desire.

All this could be cured by exorcism. The demons could be expelled by the Christians, says Minucius; adjured by the only true God, they quake in fear in men's bodies and either come forth at once or disappear gradually, according to the strength of the faith of the sufferer or the 'grace of the healer'. It would seem that all eventualities were thus taken into account.

Even prosaic writers and philosophers acknowledged such spirits, and on at least one occasion the great Socrates admitted that he was 'instructed' by a demon. The powerful Magi, a tribe of Medians who specialized in sacred rites and traditional lore, drew their power, says Cyprian, from divination, seership, augury and astrology, for powerful demons were associated with these 'illusions', and the Magi drew on their power to work mischief.

Even so, exorcism could remove such demons, and 'by startling threats' it was possible to force the demons to confess themselves to be 'impure and vagrant' spirits that had entered 'into the bodies of men whom they purpose to destroy'. With heavy blows, these spirits could be driven out of their victims, and they would depart, howling and groaning with constantly renewed pains. The waters of baptism were said to be especially effective in the explusion of such wicked spirits, and methods that involved such holy water were known to have succeeded where all others had failed. 'By the waters of salvation and the sanctification of baptism,' Cyprian says, 'the Devil is beaten down.' In picturesque language he explains that, just as scorpions and serpents which exist on dry ground cannot live or retain their venom when cast into water, so wicked spirits could not remain in the body of a man or woman baptized and sanctified, in whom the Holy Spirit was beginning to dwell.

In baptism, a rite which was in use before the ministry of Jesus Christ commenced, the washing in water becomes the sign and symbol of inward purification from sin and uncleanness; baptism was also regarded as the symbol of resurrection from the death of trespasses and sins to a life of holiness and a participation in the future and final resurrection. Baptism, in common with exorcism, was conducted with fire as well as with water, and when the name of the Holy Ghost was invoked, fiery visitations would appear and purify the religious and destroy the wicked.

Eusebius (264–c.345), 'the father of ecclesiastical history', had little to say about exorcism, although it is obvious that he believed in the rite. Deliverance from demons can be obtained, he said, by the practice of the gospel and by chastity and a pure disposition.

Sir Shane Leslie once reminded me of the story St Gregory tells in his *Dialogues* about a ghostly deacon who haunted some baths and was seen by a bishop. He forthwith laid down that haunting spirits were of three kinds: diabolical, souls in damnation, and souls in Purgatory. He found, during his subsequent investigations (as everyone who has studied paranormal activity throughout the ages has discovered), that such ghosts or spirits could be mild, truculent or jocose, and he is perhaps the first serious investigator to observe that suicides, murderers and those who are murdered are most liable to haunt.

'But do the dead know they are haunting the living?' Sir Shane asked me, and without waiting for an answer he went on to say that it is possible they are aware but we have 'the tremendous authority' of St Thomas Aquinas (1226–74). who favours the view that the dead are not aware of their own apparitions; they may be other spirits masquerading. And this is, of course, the great difficulty facing modern spiritualism: the manifestations themselves may be genuine but the 'spirit' may not be the person it claims to be.

In 1598 the Jesuit Petrus Thyroeus published in Cologne his *Loco Infesta*, and therein he admits finding reported hauntings in many different places and at widely different times. To emphasize the orthodoxy of his belief he quotes St Augustine's story of a haunted house and of an exorcism.[1]

> Hesperius, one that has been a captain and lives at this day by us, has a little farm called Zubedi, in the district of Fussala, which having observed (by the harm done to his servants and cattle) to be haunted with evil spirits, he entreated one of our priests (in mine absence) to go thither and expel them by prayer. One went, prayed, and administered the communion, and by God's mercy the devil was driven from the place ever after....
>
> I knew a virgin in Hippo, who was freed from the devil, merely by being anointed with oil mixed with the tears of the priest that prayed for her. I know a bishop who by prayer dispossessed the devil present in a youth that he never saw....

In talking to Sir Shane Leslie, I could not help but refer to the occasional curious outbreaks of psychic activity at convents and nunneries, but Sir Shane would have none of that. 'The religious

life in thousands of convents and monasteries proceeds
normally under direction and discipline,' he said – rather
pompously, I thought, and when I began to quote chapter and
verse: the Ursuline nuns at Loudun in 1634, the Louviers
convent affair, and the school transformed into a cloister at Lisle
in Flanders in 1658, he replied, 'Only rarely from time to time are
there troubles, psychical or doctrinal …' and he related to me
the story concerning the French convent of St Pierre de Lyon
from which a sister named Alix de Telieux fled and lived a gay
life until she died – unhappily, it is said, in 1524, apparently
finding herself in Purgatory before returning as a ghost to the
convent she once knew and loved but came to detest. She
particularly seemed to pester and haunt one sister at the
convent, and her story was revealed by the time-honoured
process of raps … a story that suggested she must haunt for
many years. Eventually her body was brought back to her old
convent and buried with sacred rites, and an exorcism was
carried out by Montalembert, almoner to King Francis I.
Subsequent raps stated that the soul of Alix was saved and that
her sentence of many years of haunting had been reduced to
days. As this message came through, a mysterious and very
bright light was seen in the refectory, whereupon the nuns
retired to their chapel and sang *Te Deum*.

Moving to 1665 and back across the Channel, in January that
year the so-called Botathen Ghost manifested in Cornwall, and
we are indebted to the diary of John Rudall, a Cornish
clergyman (who acquired a reputation for dealing with ghosts),
for preserving this extraordinary story.

The story begins when Mr Rudall was approached one night
by a man named Bligh, who beseeched Mr Rudall to see his son,
who badly needed his special help. Mr Rudall accompanied
Bligh to the latter's home, an old house named Botathen in
South Petherton; there he was introduced to another clergyman,
and the three men held a council of war in the garden, out of
earshot of the son.

Mr Rudall then learned that the boy crossed a heath each day
on his way to school, and there he was constantly confronted by
the ghost of a woman in a long dress who seemed to 'swim'
along the ground. Her face was white and she looked sad and
troubled. She always had one arm hanging at her side, while the
other was stretched out in front of her. Her eyes, unblinking in

the strong sunlight, stared straight ahead. Her hair was so soft and light that it seemed almost to melt away in the brightness of the daylight.

From the boy's repeated and vivid descriptions there seemed to be no doubt but that the ghost was that of Dorothy Dinglet, a young woman who had once known the Bligh household; indeed, some three years previously she had been a constant visitor.

Rudall decided to accompany the boy next day, and sure enough they encountered the ghost gliding over the grassy heath ahead of them. The boy's spaniel whined and barked with fear and fled home from the haunted spot. Rudall afterwards admitted that he too had been more than a little startled. Having himself seen the apparition, he decided that a series of exorcisms were necessary and he approached the bishop of Exeter for the necessary permission. The bishop finally gave permission but he was not at all happy about the matter, regarding the rite of exorcism as reeking of Roman Catholic doctrines.

So, on 12 January 1665, John Rudall again visited Higher Brown Quartils (the heath's name) at the appropriate time, wearing a brass ring as a protection. He paced out and measured a circle on the grass, marked a pentacle in the centre, laid some twigs of rowan in the centre and then took up a position himself, facing north. Suddenly he heard a 'soft and rippling sound', and then he saw again the ghost of Dorothy Dinglet. With shaking hands and quaking voice, Rudall unrolled a scroll and, reading from it, commanded the ghost to enter the magic circle he had drawn. After some hesitation the ghost entered the circle and stood stationary in the centre, lowering its pointing arm for the first time. The silence must have been deafening, for ancient tradition held that a ghost could not speak unless first spoken to.

Plucking up his courage John Rudall addressed the ghost, asking it first why it could not rest – and the ghost replied that she had once committed a great sin and was bound to the earth. She then revealed something of what she had done and mentioned a name known to John Rudall; but he had to promise never to reveal that name, and in fact he honoured that pledge to the end of his days. The ghost then faded but promised to return next day.

Accordingly the following morning John Rudall was at the same place, and he then informed the ghost that since they had last met he had talked with the man 'with whom she had transgressed' and he had expressed horror and remorse and was agreeable to making atonement and accepting penance. Upon hearing this, the ghost acknowledged satisfaction, and when Rudall uttered the words of dismissal, the ghost glided towards the west and was never seen again.

One interesting note in this contemporary account of the seemingly successful exorcism of a ghost is that Rudall, on his first encounter with the ghost, was undecided as to whether he was facing a 'true spirit' or a 'false fiend', and he prudently asked for a sign that the ghost was genuine. The ghost then made a prophecy, saying that before a year had passed, '... a fearful pestilence would lay waste the land and myriads of souls would be loosened from their flesh and the valleys would be full of the dead ...', thereby prophesying, it seems, the great plague of 1665.

The diary of John Rudall's experiences was re-written, incidentally, by no less a writer than Daniel Defoe. Perhaps a little sadly it has to be said that, in spite of John Rudall's convincing story of the exorcism of the ghost of Dorothy Dinglet, it has reportedly been seen on a number of occasions over the years.

Advancing 200 years, we encounter Daniel Dunglas Home, to some the greatest of all spiritualist charlatans, to others the most outstanding of all spiritualist mediums. What cannot be disputed is that he is the most famous medium of all time, that he was never caught cheating in many years of mediumship in many parts of the world and that he accepted no payment for his sittings. Not only was he never exposed but no valid explanation of his methods and seeming miracles has ever been given or even suggested. Among his apparent gifts was exorcism. While he was on one of his visits to Italy, a British woman in Florence asked him whether he could exorcize a troublesome ghost. Calling on the name of the Holy Spirit, he succeeded in banishing the ghost. For a while it rapped intermittently, all over the house, and then it departed for ever.

Jean Burton, in her biography of the remarkable medium Daniel Dunglas Home, states: 'There had been ... that surprising episode at Genoa when Dickens rescued an

Englishwoman from the unwelcome attentions of a phantom, by exorcism ...' I think my knowledgeable friend Renée Haynes, Council Member of The Society for Psychical Research, must be right on this curious entry. Over tea at my cottage in Hampshire I asked Renée about this 'exorcism', which I knew nothing about, and she said she recalled an incident involving mesmerism and possibly there was a misprint in Miss Burton's book.

I went to John Foster's *Life of Charles Dickens* (Everyman's Library edition, 1966) where I read '... Mrs De la Rue (the English wife of a Swiss banker) suffered from attacks of frightening hallucinations, and from time to time Dickens ministered to her, apparently with some success, by mesmeric treatment.' So I think that must be the answer, and there was no 'exorcism', as such, performed by Charles Dickens.

Advancing another hundred years we find a report in June 1988 of a Kenyan Evangelical pastor, John Kimutai Korir, whose attempted exorcism of a 17-year-old girl went sadly wrong. According to Associated Press reports at the time, his attempts to exorcize an evil spirit from the girl culminated in his cutting out her lungs before he and others members of the sect went to a house to pray for her. Korir was eventually gaoled for three years for killing the girl. He denied murdering Jane Chepkeomoi but admitted unintentional manslaughter.

A couple of years earlier the Rev. Michael Bunce had attempted to exorcize the ghost that was troubling a house in Heathfield Road, Grantham. Nicknamed 'Charlie', this ghost reportedly not only moved objects, disturbed the controls on a cooker and even nailed the lodger's trousers to the ceiling but was heard singing the current pop songs and once told landlady Harriet Weller when she admolished him for disturbing everyone: 'Shut up, woman!'

After visiting the house Mr Bunce reportedly said: 'I distinctly heard a deep voice in the hallway suddenly say, "This is Charlie."' He added, 'I think there must be something there – and it is completely beyond my understanding.'

I am reminded of a case in Grimsby where the visiting clergyman was equally puzzled; a case that was visited by two Ghost Club investigators in an attempt to help the family. In fact, no fewer than four priests visited the house on one occasion, carrying candles and a cross in an attempt to vanquish the entity that brought terror to the household; an exorcism we will examine in some detail in Chapter 8.

Dom Robert Petitpierre – of whom we shall hear more later – once told me of a quite remarkable case of haunting that he successfully exorcised. In the East End of London a home for girls was opened in premises that had once been a brothel, and every night one of the girls housed there 'went off the rails' sometimes within a few weeks of arriving. Not unnaturally this startling sexual activity worried everyone connected with the home, and the parish priest was called in. He decided that the girls were under evil influences left behind when prostitution flourished in the building, and he felt the place should be exorcised.

Dom Robert Petitpierre told me he talked with the priest and with a Roman Catholic bishop who was called in to conduct a service of exorcism; in fact he attempted to carry out several services of release and two full exorcisms but he broke down each time, feeling that an overwhelming force was against him and he could make no headway.

Then an exorcism with the bishop and twelve clergymen was conducted, including Dom Robert, and this 'cleared the mess up', as he put it. The house was all right afterwards. Many cases of haunting suggest that something of previous occupants can remain in a house after people depart, a 'something' that occasionally manifests either independently or in association with a member or members of the incoming family; it is an influence that usually soon disintegrates and disappears. Something like this may have happened at the East End home for girls but it is interesting to note that persistent exorcism seemed to clear the property.

As recently as April 1988 the Rev. Robert Law, one of the bishop of Truro's officially appointed 'adversaries of the occult', talked about his work. Perhaps surprisingly, he admitted that he had never seen a ghost, and he was, he said, much more concerned with those he believes are haunted by their own guilt or by living relatives.

I found myself in complete agreement with this vicar of Crowan, Cornwall, when he said, 'There is nothing to fear from a haunting. It is often a cry for help.' I could not agree when he went on to say, 'There is a power of evil beyond our own making, and it uses people for all sorts of minor acts of evil.'

That seems to me to be a complete contradiction of his previous statement.

One interesting case that the Rev. Robert Law talked about concerned 'an abnormal coldness' and, as he rightly pointed out, one sign of a haunting is an inexplicable, definite and measurable drop in temperature.

Mr Law visited a bungalow in Cornwall where one room was always four or five degrees colder than the rest of the house. 'It had been the home of an old lady who died there because she did not want to ever leave the place. The property was to be passed to relatives with whom she had fallen out and they took her body out of the bungalow, but I am certain some part of her stayed there,' the Rev. Robert Law stated.

After he had 'blessed' the bungalow, the temperature returned to normal and the house 'stayed the same afterwards'. Oddly enough the householder's daughter was using a video recorder during the clergyman's requiem for the dead woman, and it was found that at the time he was conducting his blessing, the tape wiped itself clean – and that the magnetic structure of the tape had been so changed that it was no longer possible to record on the tape. Subsequently this tape was checked by an engineer, who was totally unable to explain what had happened to it.

2   Some Curious Exorcisms

During the course of research for this book, I discovered that there have been some very curious exorcisms over the years, and in fact there is nothing new in somewhat strange attempts at exorcism in strange places. As long ago as 1810 a family plagued by strange happenings resorted to using a sword and a Bible. The Rev. Caleb Colton, who had personal experience of the strange disturbances, recounted the full story in his *Narrative of the Sampford Ghost*. An old house at Sampford Peverell in Devon became the target for what has been described as a classic poltergeist infestation. Certainly a great variety of happenings that seemed to show a considerable degree of skill were reported by a variety of witnesses.

In a house occupied by Mr John Chave, he, his family and his servants all had personal experience of the poltergeist; indeed the women of the house were reportedly beaten black and blue! As with most poltergeist infestations, the initial incidents were the easiest to explain. They consisted of the sound of footsteps (the commonest of all reported phenomena in haunted houses), as though an unseen presence was walking about the house; when little notice was taken of these sounds, they increased in quantity and intensity until it seemed that '... the chambers of the house were filled, even in daylight, with thunderous noises and upon any persons stamping several times on the floors of the upstairs rooms, they would find themselves imitated – only much louder – by the upstairs agency!'

Mr Colton states that when the female members of the household were being beaten as they slept by some unseen presence – and he heard upwards of 200 violent blows in one night being delivered – the sounds resembled that of a strong man striking with all his might with his clenched fists. One of the young servant girls, Ann Mills, had a black eye and a swelling as big as a turkey's egg on her cheek. Two of the other women servants, Mary Dennis and young Mary Woodbury, swore that they were beaten by something invisible until they were numb with the pain and were sore for days afterwards.

When the servants were too frightened to use the bedroom in which they had been so cruelly mistreated, Mr and Mrs Chave invited them to share their bedroom. Soon violent disturbances were taking place there too, night after night, with candles and candlesticks hurtling about the room of their own volition and curtains around the fourposters shaking violently, to the horror of the occupants. Once Mr Chave narrowly missed being hit on the head when a huge iron candleholder came hurtling at him. The Rev. Caleb Colton says he '... often heard the curtains of the bed being violently agitated, accompanied by a loud and almost indescribable motion of the rings. These curtains, four in number, were, to prevent their motion, often tied up, each in one large knot. Every curtain of that bed was agitated and the knots thrown and whirled about with such rapidity that it would have been unpleasant to be within the sphere of their action. This lasted about two minutes and concluded with a noise resembling the tearing of linen; Mr Taylor and Mr Chave of Mere, being also witnesses. Upon examination a rent was found across the grain of a strong new cotton curtain.'

The disturbances continued for eight months, with raps, knockings, rattling noises and a 'sound like that of a man's foot in a slipper coming downstairs and passing through a wall' being repeatedly experienced. Once the Rev. Caleb Colton was in the act of opening a door when there was a violent rapping on it, seemingly from the other side. Colton paused without opening the door, and the rapping came again; taking his courage in both hands, suddenly he opened the door and peered out, candle in hand, but there was nothing to see. Sometimes these noises were so loud and violent that the occupants, Mr Colton and anyone else present, really thought that the walls and ceilings would collapse.

Among the score of independent witnesses of the Sampford Ghost (as it came to be called) and a number of affidavits sworn out before magistrates, there is Mr Searle, the governor of the county gaol, a no-nonsense, down-to-earth man who came to see for himself the strange happenings, and he attempted a rather odd exorcism of the disturbances.

He had brought with him a sword (no doubt to tackle any earthly agent of the 'ghost') and, satisfied that the disturbances were not of this world, he attempted to exorcize the ghost by the curious expedient of placing the heavy sword at the foot of the bed in the room where the disturbances were most frequent and at a time when the happenings were at their height, and on top of the sword he placed a weighty folio Bible. Within seconds both sword and Bible were flung through the air, and both of them crashed against the opposite wall, several feet away.

Another visitor, a Mr Taylor (already referred to), was in the house at the time but not in the particularly 'haunted' room with the governor; when he heard shrieks coming from the bedroom, he hurried upstairs and entered the room and was just in time to see the sword suspended in mid-air and pointing towards him! Almost immediately and in view of everyone present, it then clattered heavily to the floor.

As with many poltergeist infestations, the disturbances ceased as mysteriously and as suddenly as they had begun, although not before rumours of conscious fraud and criticism of the Rev. Caleb Colton began to circulate in the area. The criticism against Mr Colton, for his participation in the affair, seems unfair on the face of it, for it is not generally known that he contributed £100 from his own pocket (a considerable sum in those days) to the £250 on offer to anyone who could give such information as might lead to a discovery of the answer to the mysterious events at Sampford Peverell.

Although the money was never claimed, years later it was discovered that the old house had double walls, with a passage between them, which could have assisted conscious trickery; and there was the distinct possibility that the premises were at one time used by smugglers who might have encouraged the 'weird' noises for their own purposes – and, of course, many a pastor in days gone by was known to help local smugglers. On the other hand, Eric Maple reports that a living descendant of one of the owners of the house, destroyed by fire nearly fifty years ago, still insists that the hauntings were undoubtedly genuine.

Among attempted exorcisms involving a large Bible is one associated with Spedlin's Tower near Lockerbie in Scotland. Here, it has been said, a most unpleasant ghost terrified the countryfolk hereabouts for centuries.

The story goes that many, many years ago the laird of Applegirth was Sir Alexander Jardine, the first baronet. All that now remains of Jardine Hall stands opposite ruined Spedlin's Tower. Sir Alexander had occasion to punish a miller named Porteous whose cottage had burnt down, and this the laird did by confining the unfortunate man in the dungeon of the tower.

Sir Alexander had to go to Edinburgh in a great hurry, and in his haste he took with him the only key to the dungeon. As soon as he discovered what he had done, he sent the key back, but it was too late: the unlucky miller had died of starvation. In fact, it is said that the dying man was so ravaged by hunger that he had gnawed at his own hands and feet in the last throes of torment.

Soon after the miller's death Sir Alexander's household began to be plagued by the ghostly form of the poor Porteous. A loud battering noise would be heard, night after night, on the door of the dungeon, and a hollow voice would call piteously: 'Let me out ... let me out ... I'm dying of hunger ...' When mischievous children of the household inserted a stick through the keyhole, it is said that the hungry ghost stripped the bark from the stick in an instant!

The aid of the local clergy was invoked and a ritual of exorcism performed in which a large 'black-lettered' Bible was left in a niche by the dungeon doorway. This seemed to placate the ghost, but years later, when the Bible was temporarily removed for rebinding, the ghost, it seems, returned.

By this time, however, the Jardine family had moved to their new residence on the other side of the River Annan, and for a time the ghost is reported to have followed, entering the baronet's bedroom and creating such a noise and disturbance that no time was lost restoring the Bible to its place, whereupon peace was restored. When the Jardine family eventually sold the hall and tower, they left the Bible to prevent the ghost from roaming, although there are to this day sporadic reports of Porteous's voice calling to be released from the crumbling Spedlin's Tower.

Incidentally I mentioned the haunting of Spedlin's Tower and the Jardine family in my *Gazetteer of Scottish and Irish Ghosts*, and a reader was kind enough to send me a contemporary report from a local paper headed, 'My Precious Book: Bible protects Sir William from angry ghost ...' The report reads:

A Dumfriesshire landowner lives with a haunting fear of the return of a family ghost and to protect his family Lt. Col. Sir William Jardine of Applegirth, Bart., OBE, TD, DL, who lives at Denbie House near Dalton, keeps a mediaeval bible as one of his most treasured possessions. Sir William spoke of his 'genuine belief' that the centuries-old bible, handed down to him by his ancestors, protects him and his family from being harassed by the ghost of the angry miller. From the time of the original disturbances, around 1540, the bible has been the most closely guarded possession of the Jardines.

After relating the ghost story Sir William was asked (in 1980) whether he seriously believed in the bible's power to keep the ghost away. 'I certainly do', he replied, 'after all, how would you like to be haunted?' The bible, which is always kept under lock and key in a Thornwood box, will eventually be passed on to Sir William's eldest son, Alexander, who lives in Oxford, thus protecting yet another generation of Jardines.

A further piece in the same local newspaper stated that Lady Jardine shared her husband's views on the 'exorcizing' power of the Bible, and a local man named Harkness who had once been a gardener at Jardine Hall stated that he had fished near Spedlin's Tower on many occasions and, although he had never seen the ghost, he admitted that on one particular occasion a chilling feeling came over him, and he said, 'I could not have stayed there – not for a thousand pounds.' It can be quite eerie near the tower, especially around midnight, when the clock in the tower at Jardine Hall chimes the witching hour. Most local people and those who knew the story are more than prepared to accept that the Bible has some mysterious power, and in this case it has the power to exorcize the ghost of the Jardines.

Exorcism, for more than 500 years, has attracted priests and others to try their hands in various ways against evil spirits. There was even a madman, named Arthur Hackett, who professed himself not only an exorcist but the Messiah himself, and he ended his days by being summarily hanged! Other would-be exorcists claimed to entice evil spirits into bottles, where they were securely corked and formally banished to the Red Sea for 999 years. It all seems a far cry from religious exorcism and the freeing of tortured spirits.

In at least one guide to the supernatural in the British Isles, Calverley Hall, north of Bradford in Yorkshire, is described as being haunted by the ghost of Walter Calverley. In another volume on the British supernatural scene, the same ghost is credited with also haunting two churches. Be that as it may, the story of Walter Calverley and a ritual of exorcism that was conducted is worthy of examination.

Walter Calverley seems to have inherited more than wealth and fortune from the ancient Catholic family that could trace its pedigree back for many centuries, for he was undeniably insane and on 23 April 1604 he ran amok and stabbed to death two of his children and all but murdered his wife, whose life was saved by her protecting corset. He thought he had killed her and set off to find and kill his remaining son, Henry. Fate intervened as the reckless and wild rider, soon being pursued at full speed, was thrown from his horse. He was captured, brought to trial at York and, when he refused to plead, sentenced to death by pressing. Still refusing to plead, Walter Calverley died under a great weight of stones and was buried at St Mary's Castlegate, York, although later, it is said, his body was secretly transferred to the family vault at Calverley.

This does not seem to have affected the reputation that St Mary's churchyard soon acquired – that of being haunted by the ghost of Walter Calverley. Soon Calverley Hall too was being haunted by the same ghost, and there were stories of Walter Calverley's desperate last ride being re-enacted time and time again. Sometimes the spectral rider would be seen, followed by a band of mounted phantoms, leaving Calverley churchyard and racing through the countryside – without making a sound.

At Calverley Hall the ghost of Walter Calverley was seen and felt by various people, including the Rev. Richard Burdsall, who found himself awake in the middle of the night with the feeling of an intolerable weight on his chest – and he was hurled from his bed no fewer than three times! Only afterwards did he learn about Walter Calverley's being pressed to death.

One way and another, things became so bad that the local priest was called in to exorcize the ghost, and he did the best he could, banishing the ghost of Walter Calverley with the injunction that it was not to reappear 'as long as hollies grew green in Calverley Wood ...' but this exorcism was singularly unsuccessful, and it has been suggested that the strange rites of exorcism may be effective against the spirits of sane men but have little influence when the ghost is that of a madman!

Another interesting but apparently unsuccessful exorcism comes from Wales and concerns the redoubtable Owen Glendower (c.1360–c.1416), whose ghost is one of those reputed to appear whenever the country is in danger. Glendower is said to have killed the Welsh chieftain Howel Sele at Nannau, and afterwards he hid the bleeding corpse inside a blasted oak tree. Soon the area around this tree came to be regarded as haunted by Howel Sele's ghost, although it was not until long afterwards that the tree was cut open and the bleached corpse came to light. Burial rites were read for the dead chieftain, Masses were said for his soul, exorcisms were carried out on the spot but still the area was haunted.

During the course of a visit to Wales when I was researching my book *Ghosts of Wales*, my wife and I found noble Nannau Old Hall, former seat of the Vaughan family, nestling in wooded countryside 800 feet above sea-level, and we talked with the owner, Mr E.A. Morrison, who showed us round the quite fascinating and historic house that he had lovingly restored.

The original mansion belonged to Howel Sele, first cousin to Owen Glendower, who claimed to be able to 'call spirits from the vasty deep'. The cousins really hated one another, and at one time the abbot of Kymmer, hoping to bring about a reconciliation between the kinsmen (according to the historian Pennant), arranged for a meeting between the two men at Nannau. Outwardly the cousins were amiable enough, and the abbot congratulated himself that he had achieved his aim. There at historic Nannau, with its history and memories, all would be well, he told himself; why, already the two men were out walking together.

They were indeed, but when Owen espied a doe feeding, he pointed out the animal to Howel, who was considered to be an exceptional archer, and said he doubted whether Howel could kill the creature at such a distance.

Howel appeared to take up the challenge. He bent his bow and, pretending to take aim at the doe, suddenly turned and discharged the arrow full at the breast of Owen Glendower, who, however, had foreseen something of the kind and was wearing armour beneath his tunic and so was not much hurt. He was enraged at this treachery and set about evening the score.

One dark night he stole up to Howel Sele's home and set the place on fire. When Howel rushed out to get help, Owen set about him and carried him off in the confusion. Nothing of

Howel was seen for forty years, but then, when he was on his death bed, Owen Glendower related to his faithful companion, Madog, what had really happened and where he had hidden the body.

As soon as Glendower was dead, Madog hurried to Nannau to inform Howel Sele's ever-hopeful wife that she was in fact a widow, and he was able to reveal to her where her husband's body had lain hidden for all those years. Leading the widow and her men to a great oak tree, Madog told them to tear it open. When this was done, a large, bleached skeleton was revealed, of the same approximate height and build as Howel Sele. Full burial rites and a family funeral were held in the sad house of Nannau, but soon stories of the ghost of the murdered man began to circulate. Time after time the fearful bleeding ghost was seen by people passing the place after dark, and sometimes the singular ghost was reported by strangers who had no knowledge of it or the reputed haunting.

Over the years, things became so bad that it was felt a service of exorcism must be held for the unquiet ghost, and when even these measures proved unsuccessful in laying it, an exorcism to end all exorcisms was, I have been told, carried out.

It seems that the local clergy, abbots, bishops and canons, aggrieved and humiliated that their sacred power could not help the noble house in their midst, decided upon a course of action that they were sure would be powerful enough to overthrow any evil force.

The story goes that no fewer than forty clergymen with forty bells, forty candles, forty crucifixes, forty vessels of holy water and forty Bibles, carried out forty exorcisms for forty hours and then retired exhausted. And all for nothing, or so it would seem, for there continued to be stories of dreadful sights and sounds around Nannau after darkness fell, and the awful spectre of the murdered Howel was still reportedly seen.

Maybe there was no 'spirit' of Howel to exorcize, just the harmless shade of something that had happened long ago, impressed upon the atmosphere to return or to be seen under certain conditions, a kind of atmospheric-photograph ghost that is there to be seen by anyone if they are in the right place at the right time. This kind of ghost usually eventually runs down, almost like a battery; perhaps there is or was something exceptional about the ghost of Howel Sele or perhaps his ghost has at last run its course, for I have had no reports of its being seen recently.

On the lawn at Nannau there used to be a sundial which carried an inscription on a brass plate and a representation of an oak tree, marking the spot where the tree once stood where the probable body of Howel remained for forty years before it was discovered, too late for the perpetrator of the evil deed to be punished. For years it was said that on certain nights of the year a great oak tree would replace the sundial, and for a few brief moments the air would be filled with hate and menace and the harsh breathing of a man, almost as though he was struggling to hide a heavy burden within the ample confines of the gigantic tree; then all would be quiet and still; the tree would disappear and in its place the peaceful sundial would stand again for all to see and wonder.

A curious form of exorcism was explained to me by Nina Epton, who encountered it in Morocco where it was used to chase away devils from the house of a prospective bride. Nina told me that the memory that lingered longest from all her Moroccan travels was the sound of the long, double iron spoons of the Gnaoua or Demon Dancers: wild and primeval, as they troop along dark alleys at dead of night, dispelling whispering spirits and invisible ghosts by the means of music and incantation.

Visiting a prospective bridegroom, Nina Epton was startled to hear a 'weird pot-and-pan noise' outside the house, like metal castanets but louder and more imperious. The bridegroom paused in his chat with her, listened and then a frown flashed across his face. 'There are the Gnaoua,' he said. 'I must go down.' And he was away down the stairs to welcome them.

There were seven Gnaoua and a child, a wizened, hollow-eyed little boy of six or seven years disguised as a man. The leader and the drummer were the only members to wear a red fez, distinguishing them from the other devil-exorcizers. The leader took no part in the dancing, conversing with the bridegroom and other members of the household, casually smoking and taking his ease while his dancers went through a frenzied performance in which nobody appeared to be in the least interested. Doubtless they had seen it all before; another routine exorcism ritual, taken for granted.

The dancers pirouetted as the musicians played their raucous music; they twirled in circles, they leaped and bounded with frantic energy but impassive countenances. The drummer did no dancing; a silent, sinister figure, he dominated the group, playing incessantly on his large drum with curved drumsticks. The drum was decorated all over with strange, magic symbols, and the drummer had a secret, far-away look on his face; he hardly seemed to notice his companions as they whirled and sped round and round him.

Once they decided that they had chased away from the bridegroom's house the main body of devils with their ear-splitting din, the Gnaoua filed out and surrounded the bridegroom's car, for envious spirits would endeavour to accompany him on his way to his bride's house.

Meanwhile another procession of Gnaoua advanced on the house of the bride, led by a curious character continuously blowing a slim flute at least five feet in length. He repeatedly blew it towards the four points of the compass and then lowered the instrument until it appeared to be sniffing the ground like an elephant's trunk; it was in fact searching for djinns and spirits of an evil nature. Apparently satisfied that he had rid the place of evil spirits, the flute-player disappeared into the shadows and was not seen again.

Nina Epton told me that in Morocco the Gnaoua dance to dispel devils, while the Aissaoua dance to liberate the possessed, to expel devils – those same Aissaoua who are known for their violent side evidenced by tearing to pieces live sheep, but then the Aissaoua are the inheritors of the terrible Dionysiac dismemberment rites of ancient Greece – but that is another story. The Aissaoua are able to transmit divine healing and blessing: a beneficial influence that they believe is transmitted by a dead or living saint that cures the possessed person.

Sir Shane Leslie told me about a very different method of releasing a possessed person that he had come across from South Africa. A girl in a convent there was believed to have sold herself to the Devil in return for gifts which she coveted. She revealed this state of affairs by seemingly being possessed. The nuns took the remarkably speedy advance in her studies as a compliment to their teaching, until she took to flying about the place without visible means of support and showing all the signs of being possessed.

The bishop was consulted and decided that the signs were unmistakable and warranted exorcism. He prepared himself for the ordeal by prayer and fasting and then went to the church and summoned the girl. She was extremely reluctant to enter the church and seemed to know what was afoot; something inside her expressed itself with all kinds of reasons and excuses for not entering the church at that time, and it took over an hour for her to be persuaded and induced and cajoled into entering the holy place and approaching the bishop, to whom, at length, she confessed her ambitious attempt to deal with a malevolent power. Then, suddenly, she collapsed and was reunited happily with her kind.

Lay techniques were very different, as we have seen, and involved such practices as drinking holy waters from upturned church bells or holding the patient's head over a bowl of burning brimstone until his or her face was black with smoke. Sometimes, as we have also seen, a holy relic would be introduced into the proceedings without warning, and unceremoniously thrust into the affected person's body.

Sometimes 'devils' were actually reported to be driven out of the bodies they were seemingly occupying by some such powerful exorcisms, and not a few leading Church dignitaries became famous for exorcisms they conducted and carried out. St Zeno, Bishop of Verona for ten years in the fourth century, is credited with such powers, and the panels of the church of San Zeno, Verona, depict scenes from the Bible and miracles and exorcisms attributed to the bishop, whose body still resides in a glass case inside the church. One panel clearly shows St Zeno exorcizing a woman by driving a large and sexless demon from her mouth, while she is held by an assistant. Understandably the patient is wide-eyed at the sight of the demon emitted from her!

A very different exorcism was carried out by the Rev. Donald Omand at Kettleness near Scarborough when he heard from a schoolmaster who had experienced a brooding evil at a desolate stretch of country where another man had reported seeing a phantom hound.

Dracula devotees will recall that Bram Stoker refers to doom-laden Kettleness and the great black dog that was seen there. Omand was aware that Stoker knew this stretch of the Yorkshire coast, and he believed that the writer had also seen the phantom hound and that the sight had so fired his imagination that he had originated the sinister Count Dracula and his landing there as a black hound.

At all events Omand visited Kettleness with the schoolmaster, and suddenly they both saw the form of a huge black hound that was 'surely not of this world'. It moved towards them, and the schoolmaster rushed back to his car but exorcist Donald Omand was made of sterner stuff. He felt that the manifestation was something evil, and he proceeded to deal with it as he had dealt with evil many times before.

He had come prepared and, uncorking a bottle of holy water, he commenced to address the spectre: 'Be gone in the name of the Lord Jesus Christ. Be gone to the place appointed for you, there to remain for ever. Be gone in the name of Christ.' As he spoke these words, he splashed holy water in the direction of the apparition, which disappeared as suddenly as it had appeared. Donald Omand then exorcized all the ground where the phantom hound had appeared, and he felt a great heaviness lift from the atmosphere there. He came away utterly convinced that the menace of Kettleness was ended and that the corruption that had been there had departed.

The redoubtable Dr Alexander Cannon, whose book *The Power Within* inspired Morey Bernstein, author of *The Search for Bridey Murphy*, to start his study of reincarnation, claimed to have exorcized a powerful curse. At a Ghost Club meeting he revealed that, while visiting a temple at Luxor in Egypt a certain titled gentleman and his wife found some kind of religious scene in progress, with those taking part wearing wreaths of roses on their heads and reciting curious incantations and performing curious rites. As the visitors wandered about the temple, their presence and movements appeared to distract the worshippers, one of whom requested that they leave the temple, but the titled Englishman refused to do so, pointing out that the temple was open to the public and that he and his wife had as much right to be there as anyone else.

It transpired that the sect of worshippers were in fact black magicians, and they were conducting a ceremony of worship to Isis, to whom the Luxor temple is dedicated. As the couple continued their exploration of the temple, the worshippers became restive, and again one of their number requested that they leave. A rather heated argument followed, and this upset her ladyship, who became uneasy and decided to leave the temple. Her husband, however, was determined to remain as long as he wished and, having with him a cine-camera, he began to photograph the proceedings. This so infuriated the worshippers that their priest interrupted the service and advancing upon the Englishman solemnly cursed him and his family for ever.

A few months later the visiting Englishman's second son was killed in a street accident, and seven months later his wife was killed in an air crash. Three weeks previously his little nephew died during an operation, and the next year his father died. Within a year or two there was scarcely a member of the family who had not been affected by illness or death.

Several times the Englishman tried to get in touch with the sect to see whether he could make his peace and ask for the curse to be removed, but the worshippers seemed to have scattered all over the world and there appeared to be no plans for them to revisit Egypt, and so he was unsuccessful. He then contacted Dr Cannon and begged for any assistance he could give him.

Dr Cannon told him the curse *would* be removed, since a petition to God never failed; was it not written, 'Whatsoever ye ask the Father in My name, He will give unto you'? Dr Cannon solemnly 'telepathized' to the black magician who had issued the curse, the words of Isaiah: 'My word shall not return unto me void, but shall accomplish that whereunto it is sent.' He added the words: 'To those who cursed this nobleman in that Luxor temple: thye word shall return unto thee, and the curse which thou hast placed upon the head of this most noble and respected lord, now returns to thee and lies upon thine own head and upon thine own house! Curses, like chickens, come home to roost.'

Later Dr Cannon heard that the curse had apparently been lifted, and the lord wrote to him to say that a weight had been lifted from him, and he and his family were prospering.

Among other strange exorcisms carried out by the Rev. Dr Donald Omand was an attempt to cleanse the Bermuda Triangle, that area of ocean marked by Bermuda, Florida and Puerto Rico where at least 200 lives have been lost in seemingly inexplicable circumstances – usually the victims are passengers and crew of aeroplanes or ships that simply disappear. Omand's attempt to purge this huge area was, he felt, the ultimate challenge for his power as an exorcist, for he believed that the area was tainted by an ancient curse.

Taking with him Dr Terry Glanvill and author Marc Alexander, Dr Omand set up his headquarters at Elbow Beach Hotel in Bermuda. From there he planned a service of exorcism followed by a 'blessing of the waters', while at the same time prayers would be said at the three points of the Triangle. The day before the appointed day the Anglican bishop of Bermuda, the Rt. Rev. Anselm Genders, visited the exorcist and provided him with a wafer of the host and some special holy water from the shrine of Walsingham. Once the bishop had left, Donald Omand performed a service of holy communion to protect all those taking part.

Next morning at a prearranged time the service of exorcism was carried out, the exorcist holding open the book containing passages he had specially written for this unique exorcism. He followed his usual procedure at first but at the preliminary intercession his prayer included the words: 'Grant that by the power entrusted to thy unworthy servants this immense stretch of water and the lands adjoining may be delivered from the spirit of evil, all vain imaginations, projections, phantasms, paranormal magnetism and all deceits of the evil one. O Lord of all mercy, forgive the deeds of darkness committed on these waters in days gone by, and remove for ever the dark legacy of punishment invoked in desperation by sorely afflicted children in captivity ...'

Next came the cleansing ceremony, the Mozarabic prayer (an ancient liturgy used by the Christians of Toledo) and the final invocation, after which Donald sprinkled the holy water three times, and so completing the exorcism, he announced that he was sure it had been successful – or, as he put it, 'The demon has gone to his appointed place and henceforth shall bring no sorrow to the children of men.' Donald Omand then walked into the clear waters of Horseshoe Bay and blessed the waters to round off the exorcism.

Twelve days after the exorcism all the three engines of a Boeing 727 on a flight from Miami to Newark suddenly stopped and the aircraft plunged over 7,000 feet. But then, as suddenly and as mysteriously as they had ceased to function, the engines restarted, and what would undoubtedly have been another

Bermuda Triangle disaster was averted. Why on this occasion did the interference with the aeroplane's engines cease after only five minutes? Donald Omand had no doubt: his exorcism had been successful.

'Deep sea fishermen accept the supernormal (they call it the supernatural) and all that may emanate from it,' one exorcist told me, and the Rev. Tom Willis would agree. In 1987 he was called in by the Department of Health and Social Security after a senior official was puzzled by the fact that the skipper and crew of the trawler *Pickering* were always claiming dole money for being out of work when the fishing trawler appeared to be in perfect condition. He was told, 'We believe the trawler is haunted.'

Stories had spread that not only had a ghostly figure been seen on the deck of the trawler late at night but the steering would go wrong suddenly, sending the trawler round and round in circles; time after time at 1.30 in the morning the radio would malfunction; lights on the trawler would go on and off for no apparent reason, and some of the cabins were always freezing cold, even with the heating turned up full. The ghostly figure which had reportedly been seen on deck late at night appeared to be quite solid and acted naturally; it wore a flat cap and was dressed like a trawlerman, but it disappeared in circumstances that could not be rationally explained. One crew member who saw the figure asked for a transfer to another trawler when he also experienced unexplained engine failure on the trawler – twice, at night, far out at sea. He left, but engineers who examined the engines said they could find nothing wrong with them.

The Rev. Tom Willis was sufficiently intrigued by the whole matter to look into the history of the trawler, and he found that the boat came originally from Ireland, being registered in County Cork as *The Family Crest*. He also discovered that a man had been lost overboard when the trawler was owned by a family named Gallegher. The vicar decided to exorcize the trawler.

Having prepared himself and taking with him that which he considered necessary, the Rev. Tom Willis put to sea in Bridlington Bay with skipper Derek Gates and the rest of the crew. Once well clear of land, the vicar visited every part of the trawler, sprinkling holy water and calling on any restless spirit to depart. That completed, he held a service of exorcism on deck, and all on board joined him in prayer.

The next day, according to Skipper Gates, a very different atmosphere was sensed by everyone. For the fist time, as far as they could remember, there was a warm and friendly feeling on the trawler, and since then there have been no problems – and some very successful fishing trips! The Rev. Tom Willis told me he believed the restless spirit on board the trawler had found peace, and on that happy note this particular exorcism ends.

Another odd exorcism was carried out at Loch Ness. Over the years there have been so many well-established sightings of something at Loch Ness that it would be a foolish person who denies that there was no mysterious animal or unusual influence there.

The late Ted Holiday, who was convinced that he had seen the so-called 'monster' on three occasions, came to the conclusion that the famous lake monsters were not some kind of unknown species or prehistoric survivor, as thought by Sir Peter Scott, but rather a projection from the human unconscious, not a thing of flesh and blood at all; psychical rather than physical – a spectre of something that existed in these waters in the long-forgotten past. This somewhat eccentric view that some influence was at work, not only to project the image of a lake monster but also actively to prevent the solution to the mystery, was shared by, among others, the Rev. Donald Omand, whom we have already met.

Omand seemed to possess 'second sight', the ability to foretell future events, to discern occurrences at distant places and to perceive things not visible to ordinary sight, possibly inherited from his Highland ancestors. As a clergyman of the old school, he entertained no doubts as to the very real existence of the power of evil, and he was used to performing exorcisms to get rid of such 'mischief', as he called it. He had seen lake monsters at Loch Long in Ross-shire and on the eerie Norwegian Fjord of the Trolls, where the monster had also been seen at the same time by the captain of the fishing boat on which they were travelling.

After correspondence and discussion, Holiday and Omand (who had consulted his fellow-exorcist the Rev. Dom Robert Petitpierre on the matter) joined forces and carried out preliminary exorcism at four points of an imaginary cross encompassing the long waterway, and where the vertical and horizontal lines of the cross intersected, in the middle of the loch, Omand performed the final rite of exorcism. He was also careful to make a 'binding' of all evil that might be invoked at each entry or outlet to the loch and so prevent any evil departing from the loch during the exhaustive exorcism. It is not clear whether he was able to 'bind' any underwater entry to or exit from the loch.

After a brief service on the beach at Lochend, which included the application of holy water in the form of a cross on the foreheads of all the participants, the party proceeded to the four pre-arranged places on each side of the loch and at each end. Finally Omand and Holiday rowed to the centre of the loch where the final exorcism was performed, which included the words: 'I adjure thee, thou ancient serpent, by the judge of the quick and the dead, by Him who made thee and the world, that thou cloak thyself no more as manifestations of prehistoric demons, which henceforth shall bring no sorrow to the children of men.'

Readers may be interested to know that, at each part of Loch Ness where he performed his exorcism, Donald Omand used a prayer based on part of the ancient Mozarabic Rite, but adapted to Loch Ness; this reads:

> O God, the author of blessing and the Fount of salvation, we earnestly pray and beseech thee to pour the manifold dew of thy grace and the abundance of thy blessings upon this loch and the land encircling it.
>
> May Satan, the author of all evil, be driven out; may an angel of light be placed here as guardian and defender of the good; may those who come to this loch prosper and be happy and may adversity be driven out; by the multitude of thy tender mercies may peace abound for all those who sail upon these waters and upon all who dwell upon the shores adjoining this loch; may the evils of devil worship and nefarious magic cease hereabouts and may only powers and practices wholly agreeable to our Lord Jesus Christ be continued upon and around this loch.
>
> So may there always be present here, O Lord, those of thy gifts which are profitable to all men. Send, O Lord, to this loch thy good and Holy Angel as a watchman and as a sentinel and as a guard to resist evil things and provide good things for everyone here for always; so that all disquiet and disaster may be banished from this loch; may thy presence be always here and keep from this place

need, pestilence, sickness and all attacks of the evil one; so, where
thy name is invoked, may abundant good follow and may the evil
influence of the dragon be overcome and may thy protection and the
help of thy saints take its place – all this we ask in the name of the
Father, the Son and the Holy Ghost ... Amen.

Holiday stated just after the exorcism, in June 1973, that as
soon as the first introductory service had begun there was a
building-up of tension in the whole atmosphere, a distinct and
definite awareness of something very odd and strange, and this
feeling and tension built up as the exorcisms continued during
the long drive around the loch, reaching its peak at the final
exorcism, carried out in 700 feet of water in the middle of the
loch.

The instant the ceremony was completed, this tension seemed
to lift, but the Rev. Donald Omand, no longer a young man, had
found the effort exhausting and by the time the boat returned to
the bank the clergyman was completely drained and so
exhausted that he had to be carried to the caravan. He fell asleep
that night deeply content because he was certain that this
overwhelming tiredness was proof that the exorcisms had been
successful.

In the days that followed the exorcisms at Loch Ness, Donald
Omand said that reports he had received indicated that the
exorcisms had been effective, but he insisted that he had
intended to exorcize not the monster but the evil that he
believed had surrounded it, so it would not necessarily mean
that the Loch Ness monster would never be seen again; rather
that any evil which concentrated about the spectre would have
disappeared.

Subsequently, of course, Dr Robert Rines (whom I met briefly
at the funeral of Loch Ness's most famous advocate, Tim
Dinsdale, in 1987) and his team of investigators from the
Academy of Applied Science at the Massachusetts Institute of
Technology took some remarkable underwater photographs,
one of which showed something like a large flipper, while
another depicted a long-necked 'creature' and a front flipper.
These photographs were taken in conjuction with sonar
evidence – reflected waves of sound – which make it certain that
the photographed object could not be anything in the nature of
a freak shadow, floating wreckage or lake-weed. And of course
the Loch Ness monster has been reliably seen several times

since 1973 and will, I suspect, be reportedly seen again many times. During the course of the last, long conversation that my wife and I had with our valued friend of over thirty years, Tim Dinsdale told us he had no doubt about the existence of the monster, and he was sure that photographs would be obtained that would satisfy everyone, within the foreseeable future. I await that day with eagerness.

Mention of the exorcist Dom Robert Petitpierre reminds me of some of the very strange exorcisms carried out by that leading Church of England exorcist, who once told me he had banished more than a thousand ghosts and demons – or, as he called them, 'little devils'.

Dom Robert had no doubt about what he was up against. 'Real ghosts have human minds,' he used to say. 'But demons are something else. They are an army, and their general is Satan.' He believed there were spiritual beings who could decide whether they were on the side of God or not. Those who decided they were on God's side became angels and could see God; those who decided otherwise became demons and when they became troublesome could easily be exorcized.

Dom Robert Petitpierre gave evidence at the 'Forty Demons Slaughter' in Yorkshire in 1975. After a lengthy exorcism conducted by two clergymen and their lay assistant, Michael Taylor behaved irrationally and became involved with a religious sect. After an all-night exorcism, during the course of which the exorcists said they caused forty demons to leave his body, Taylor became like a wild thing and attacked his wife with 'unspeakable brutality'. He gouged out her eyes, tore out her tongue and almost tore the flesh from her face. She choked on her own blood. Taylor was found not guilty of murder because of insanity, and his counsel had some harsh things to say about exorcists and exorcism at the trial: 'We submit that those laymen who have been referred to and those clerics in particular who purported to minister to Michael Taylor on that night should be with him now in this building and each day he is incarcerated in Broadmoor.'

Dom Robert gave evidence at the inquest which followed the trial, and he told the coroner that human beings were not the only intelligences in the universe and that some of the others were definitely unpleasant, 'which is what we mean by demons'.

During the course of my many conversations with Dom Robert over the years, I was pleased to hear him say, time after time, that he always tried to explore the possibility of mental trouble before thinking about exorcism. He told me that in view of subsequent events it was clear that Michael Taylor's mental troubles had begun seriously to affect him at least a week before the exorcism that seemed to spark off the frightful murder, and it was unfortunate that those who conducted the exorcism were unaware of that situation. The result was a very real tragedy.

The possibility of human beings allegedly being posessed by 'little devils' is one thing; the attempted blessing and exorcism of animals would seem to be quite another – and perhaps it is now time to look at that curious aspect of exorcism.

3   The Exorcism and Blessing of Animals

Exorcism of haunted places and haunted people has long been practised, as we have seen, but it is a peculiar fact that from ancient records and from contemporary sources it is clear that attempts have been made to exorcise animals, including rats, caterpillars, dogs, horses and even flies! Since animals have also been allegedly cursed from time immemorial, perhaps it is not surprising that animals have also been 'blessed'.

In the Middle Ages trials of animals thought to be harmful frequently took place, trials that were conducted with all the solemnity of the law, with advocates being assigned to defend the animals. In 1457 a sow and her six young pigs were tried at Lavegny, on the charge of having killed and partially eaten a child. The sow was convicted and condemned to death, but the little pigs were acquitted on the ground of their tender years or months, the bad example of their mother, and the absence of direct evidence of their having partaken of the 'unnatural feast'.

The indictment of domestic animals for injuries inflicted on mankind was a feature of the jurisprudence of the Middle Ages, and one that was retained in the French code until the eighteenth century. Records show that ninety-two of these grotesque trials took place between 1120 and 1741, when the last one took place in Poitou.

A typical example is the case of a bull that escaped from a farmyard in 1314 in the village of Moisy, in the Valois region, and gored a man so severely that he died. It was decreed that the animal should be captured and formally prosecuted for causing the man's death. This was done, and evidence included that given by persons who had seen the bull 'deliberately escape' and by others who had seen the man 'deliberately' attacked and killed. The bull was found guilty and sentenced to

A nineteenth-century wood-carving of a devil or imp super-
imposed on Bentley church door

Armchair used by the Chinese to exorcize the possessed

Dr Alexander Cannon, who used telepathy in his exorcisms

Lawrence of Arabia's Brough Superior motorcycle, on which he had his fatal accident. The ghostly roar of this machine was successfully exorcized

Haunted Chingle Hall, Lancs., where exorcisms have been conducted to placate the unquiet ghost of John Wall

The haunted Priest Room at Chingle Hall, Lancs., where several exorcisms have failed to eradicate the ghostly activity

Historical Leith Hall, Aberdeenshire, where the present author
heard first-hand accounts of the hauntings and exorcisms

Glamis Castle, sombre and mysterious, the scene of many ghost
stories and exorcisms

Borley Rectory, Essex, long known as 'the most haunted house in England' and the subject of many exorcisms when the phenomena were at their height and for years afterwards

Harry Price, Marianne Foyster, Rev. Lionel Foyster and Kathleen M. Goldney from the Society for Psychical Research at haunted Borley Rectory in the 1930s

Algernon Blackwood (1869–1951), prolific writer and explorer of the occult, who related many tales of exorcism to the present author

Previously unpublished photograph of Harry Price and the Rev. A.C. Henning at the burial of human remains (possibly those of the Borley ghost nun) at Liston in 1945. Burial in consecrated ground has sometimes been found to be a successful form of exorcism

Guy P.J. L'Estrange, JP (*right*), who conducted a series of exorcisms at haunted Borley Rectory, talks to Ghost Club investigator Stewart Kiernander

Harry Price (1881–1948), the noted psychic investigator, who had much experience of exorcisms involving poltergeist infestations

The famous character actor Sir C. Aubrey Smith, who located a haunted house in which repeated exorcisms had been unsuccessful and who apparently manifested after his death

death, which was effected by strangulation, after which the carcase was suspended from a tree by the animal's hind legs as a warning to other animals.

A sow came to trial at Falaise in 1386 accused of tearing the face and arm of a child, causing death; and the animal was condemned to be mutilated in the head and one fore leg (as its victim had suffered) and afterwards to be strangled. This sentence was duly carried out in the public square – the unfortunate animal being dressed in a man's clothes.

In 1494 sentence of death was pronounced on a pig for having mutilated and destroyed an infant in its cradle, and the act of condemnation reads: 'We, in detestation and horror of this crime, and in order to make an example and satisfy justice, have declared, judged, sentenced, pronounced, and appointed that the said hog, being detained a prisoner, and confined in the said Abbey, shall be, by the executioner, strangled and hanged on a gibbet, near and adjoining the gallows in the jurisdiction of the said monks ... in witness of which we have sealed this present with our seal.' The document is sealed with red wax and endorsed: 'Sentence on a hog, executed by justice, brought into the copyhold of Clermont, and strangled on a gibbet at Avin.'

Three years later a sow was beaten to death for having mutilated the face of a child; and furthermore the flesh of the condemned animal was given to the dogs of the village, and the owner of the sow and his wife had to make a pilgrimage to the Church of Our Lady at Pontoise and bring back a certificate to the effect that the mission had been completed. Two years later a bull was strangled for having killed a boy – and so the records go on and on.

At Lausanne, Switzerland, in 1364, a pig that had killed a child appeared before the court, was convicted of murder and sentenced to death, the executioner being a pork butcher!

In 1474 at Basle a farmyard cock was tried on the charge of having laid an egg! It was contended that eggs laid by cocks were of 'inestimable value' for use 'in certain magical preparations', that a sorcerer would rather possess a cock's egg than the philosopher's stone and that Satan employed witches to hatch such eggs, from which winged serpents emerged which were 'most dangerous to mankind'.

By way of defence, the facts of the case were admitted but it was submitted that no evil intent had been proved and no injury to man or beast had resulted; besides, the laying of an egg was an involuntary act and as such not punishable by law. Moreover, though there was no previous record found of Satan's having possessed a 'brute creature' – a point the public prosecutor accepted – the latter suggested that, although the Evil One did not make compacts with brutes, he sometimes entered into them. He instanced the swine possessed by devils, as related by the Evangelists: the swine may have been involuntary agents, yet they nevertheless were punished by being caused to run down a steep decline into the Lake of Galilee, where they were drowned. It was all very serious, and as always the accused creature was convicted. In this case the cock was condemned to death, not as a cock but as a sorcerer or a devil who had taken the form of a cock. Accordingly the poor cock, with all the form and solemnity of a judicial execution, was burned at a stake.

In 1445 beetles caused great havoc in the vineyards of southern France, and when they reappeared in 1487 a complaint was addressed to the authorities, who ordered a judge to pronounce on the case. After evidence had been heard and an advocate had spoken on behalf of the beetles, the judge opined that the vine-growers should cede to the defendants certain land where they could live without encroaching on the vineyards. This was agreed and the judge ordered that the vineyards should be respected by the beetles, under pain of penalty. And so the farce proceeded, with claims that the land proposed to be used by the beetles was barren and with surveys and arguments proceeding almost *ad infinitum*. A perfect example, one may think, of the maxim that the only people who make anything out of litigation are the lawyers; the Italians have a saying: 'A lawyer never goes to law himself.'

A century later the inhabitants of a village in central France began legal proceedings against the rats which had infested their houses and barns, and all rats within the parish were summoned to attend trial on a named day. When no rats put in an appearance, the defence asked for an extension of time, for the summons had been addressed to old and young, sick and healthy, and certain preparations had to be made. An extension was granted but on the renewed date not a single rat put in an appearance, and it was then claimed that, although the rats were most anxious to appear in obedience to the court, they did not dare leave their homes on account of the number of cats and dogs kept by the plaintiffs in the case; if the latter would undertake to control the cats and the dogs and to pay heavy fines if the rats were molested, the summons would be immediately obeyed. While the court acknowledged the validity of this plea, the plaintiffs declined to be so bound against the good behaviour of their animals, and the case was adjourned indefinitely.

The last of these animal trials seems to have been that of a cow in a French court in 1741. Such trials, it was claimed, were founded on Jewish law, as laid down in Exodus: 'If an ox gore a man or a woman that they die, then the ox shall be surely stoned.' And the exorcizing of animals, although not having the sanction of the Mosaic law, was based on the thesis that, since God cursed the serpent, David cursed the mountains of Gilboa, and Jesus cursed the barren fig-tree, the Church had full power and authority to exorcise and excommunicate all animate and inanimate things. The first excommunication fulminated against animals is recorded in the twelfth century, when caterpillars and fieldmice were so treated, on account of the ravages they made on the crops.

So we come to the exorcism of animals. Judgement was often given in default at the trials of animals, on the non-appearance of the creature summoned, although it was generally considered that some member or members of the animal family concerned should be present when the court's decision was delivered.

In a case against leeches, tried at Lausanne in 1451, a number of leeches were brought into court to hear the document which admonished them to leave the district within three days. The leeches proved to be contumacious, did not leave the area and were consequently exorcized. This ceremony, which, we are tantalizingly told, 'deviated slightly from the recognized formula', seems to have been triumphantly successful; the leeches, immediately after the exorcism, dying off 'day by day, until they were utterly exterminated'.

The use of talismans in exorcisms has been attacked on several grounds. The French soldier Gabriel Naudé (1600–1653) ridiculed the occult virtues of talismans in his defence of Virgil (70–19BC), when the Latin poet was accused of being a magician after he cast into a well a golden talisman of a horse-leech to

drive away the great number of horse-leeches which infested
Naples. Naudé emphatically denied that the talismans
possessed any such occult virtues. It has to be regretted that so
judicious a man as Naudé should have gone to this length,
giving the lie to so many authentic authors, and it is a very
strange denial. He suspects that the thing is not true because it
is generally held to be true. 'It leads one to suspect,' he observes,
'that since animals are said to have been drawn away from so
many places by these talismans, they were ever driven from any
place.'

Whatever the pros and cons of these animal exorcisms, they
were to a considerable extent accepted, and the doctors of
Heidelberg, for example, then a famous seat of learning, gave
their entire and unanimous approbation, pointing to the
efficiency as proved by the result: the leeches had immediately
died off, after its delivery, day by day, until they were utterly
exterminated.

From the fourteenth to the sixteenth century the courts of
justice often ordered punishment on animals proportionate to
the injuries they had inflicted. Thus oxen and cows, wild or
domestic, would be killed when they were caught in the act of a
crime. Asses guilty of similar conduct were treated less harshly
and were in fact placed in the same category as thieves. The first
time that one of these animals was found in a cultivated field
which did not belong to its master, one of its ears would be cut
off. A repetition of the offence entailed the loss of the other ear.
If caught a third time in the prohibited place, the ass was
confiscated.

From the second half of the sixteenth century there are no
records of the sentence of death being passed upon animals for
homicide but a more reasonable practice condemned the owner
of the guilty animal, and he was made to forfeit damages; the
beast itself was no longer the object of a justiciary process.

In 1479 an infestation of cockchafers, a brownish beetle over an
inch in length and destructive to crops, affected the vicinity of
Lausanne. The then Chancellor of Berne advised a lawsuit
against them, and the insects were cited to appear in the
bishops' court. For counsel they had assigned to them a man
named Pessodet – who had been dead for six months! When the
accused and their advocate failed to put in an appearance, the
court gave judgment by default, and the beetles were

excommunicated '... in the name of the Holy Trinity and the Blessed Virgin and they and their descendants ...' were ordered 'to quit for ever the diocese of Lausanne'.

For many years something like a holy image was used in a number of curious cases in the Lausanne area. Once, a pig having destroyed a child, the image of St Pancras was brought out and the child was restored to life. Pancras was a Phrygian Christian who was martyred in Rome in 304, at the age of fourteen. His body was buried in the cemetery of Calepodius in Rome, and his head is preserved in the Lateran Basilica. In the Middle Ages relics of the saint were widely revered.

There is abundant evidence that charms, enchantments and exorcisms were widely used throughout Europe for the extirpation of vermin at this time. England does not appear to have enjoyed the notoriety of the legal proceedings against animals, although there is a curious case of the trial of a dog in 1771 near Chichester, while in Scotland in 1681 at Heriot's Hospital, as recorded by Lord Fountainhall, a dog was charged, found guilty of treason and actually hanged!

Berriat Saint-Prix in his *Mémoires de la Société des Antiquaries* (1829) published a list of one hundred trials of animals from 1120 to 1741, mostly from France but also from Brazil and Canada; trials that involved fieldmice, flies, snails, grasshoppers, doves, ants and worms, as well as the more common pigs, dogs, cows, sheep and ponies.

Exorcisms and the use of charms for the dispersion or destruction of noxious creatures seem to have been resorted to from a remote period, and in the Middle Ages, it was believed that certain devils had taken the form of wolves or pigs and had devoured children while in the guise of such animals. Mammet, Bishop of Vienna, had no hesitation in carrying out such exorcisms, nor had Jehan Noseret, Canon of Beaujeu, who once pronounced sentence against snails. Special talismans or charms, according to Gregory of Tours (538–c. 594), were commonly used against mice, serpents and conflagrations.

Prosecution and court action against animals were frequently carried out, as we have seen, but for country people such litigation was not only expensive but frequently tedious and diffuse, and it was not uncommon for individuals who felt themselves aggrieved by animals to purchase charms and resort to exorcisms conducted by empirical and unlicensed exorcists.

Notwithstanding the fact, if discovered, any of the parties concerned in such activity faced death by being burned at the stake, since infernal sorcerers could not presume to compete with Holy Church, there were many who were prepared to take the risk in those early days.

An exception was made in respect of one animal only, the serpent, which, as it had been cursed at a very early period in the history of the world, according to Holy Writ, could be exorcized or charmed, (so that it would leave the place where it was) by anyone, lay or cleric, without any imputation of sorcery.

An interesting account of snake-charming which has more than a touch of exorcism about it is to be found in Lane's classic, *Manners and Customs of the Modern Egyptians*, first published in 1836. Edward William Lane (1801–76) lived in Egypt from 1825 to 1849 and was the chief Orientalist of his day, and his book has been described as 'a most valuable record of Egypt's culture, its songs and legends, its folklore and superstitions; in short all that is part and parcel of Egyptian heritage'.

In discussing the snake-charmer and his methods Lane says: 'He assumes an air of mystery, strikes the walls with a short palm-stick, whistles, makes a clucking noise with his tongue, and spits upon the ground; and generally says, "I adjure you by God, if ye be above, or if ye be below, that ye come forth: I adjure ye by the most great name, if ye be obedient, come forth; and if ye be disobedient, die! die! die!" The serpent is generally dislodged by his stick, from a fissure in the wall, or drops from the ceiling of the room.'

A later formula ran: 'By Him who created thee, I adjure thee that thou remain in the spot where thou art, whether it be thy will to do so or otherwise, and I curse thee with the curse with which the Lord cursed thee.'

Exemption was only in respect of the serpent. A shepherd, long troubled by a wily and evasive wolf that plundered his sheep, was convicted as a would-be sorcerer and burned at the stake for having resorted to 'the prayer of the wolf': 'Come, beast of wool, thou art the lamb of humility! I will protect thee! Go to the right about, grey, rim and greedy beasts! Wolves, she-wolves, and young wolves, ye are not to touch the flesh which is here. Get thee behind me, Satan!'

By the seventeenth century cases of litigation against animals became fewer, although they were still practised. In the Ritual of

Evreux of 1606, for example, Cardinal Duperron of France declares that no one should exorcize animals, or use prayers or formulas against the animals, *without his express permission.* Theologians began to be aware of the problems they faced in dealing with animals, and Canon Eveillon in his *Traité des Excommunication* (1651) states: 'It is an assured theological fact that it is only a man who has been baptized that can be excommunicated.' He does not however discard exorcisms, saying they can be used towards animals, '… in the terms and ceremonies prescribed, without superstition, and not observing, as formerly, ridiculous law proceedings'.

In Spain and Italy too the lower animals were held to be subject to the law. Azpilcueta of Navarre, the distinguished Spanish theologian, asserted that rats, when exorcized, were to be ordered to depart to foreign countries, and, it is said, the obedient animals accordingly marched down in large bodies to the coast and there set off swimming in search of desert islands where they could live and enjoy themselves without annoyance to any man!

Leonard Vair, a Spanish Benedictine monk, wrote in similar vein to that of Canon Eveillon, declaring that animals are engendered from the rubbish of the earth and that submitting them to the ban of excommunication was the same as if someone baptized a dog or a stone. In fact, of course, dogs *have* been baptized – and exorcized, and stones too for that matter: in 1977 the well-known exorcist the Rev. Dr Donald Omand, whom we have already met, exorcized a prehistoric stone in Yorkshire and 'overcame its malevolence'. And in 1989 the daughter of a canon of the Church of England told me about a stone circle not far from Bath where a 'sensitive' had discovered that one stone was exuding an evil influence on people who came within its sphere. The sensitive went to some trouble to 'exorcize' the stone and is convinced that it now exerts only a beneficial influence.

There seems no end to the credulity and belief in the efficiency of such practices, and we read of similar action being taken against caterpillars, small animals and fishes, especially the large *terons* that used repeatedly to break the fishermen's nets: these creatures were annually 'banished' from the lakes and headlands of the north-west Mediterranean by Church dignitaries.

A typical exorcism would involve setting fire to part of a field's crop accompanied by an incantation on the lines of: 'Mice, caterpillars and moles, get out, get out of my field; I will burn your beard and your bones; trees and shrubs, give me three bushels of apples' – an incantation not dissimilar to the ancient formula used against flies and beetles which were thought to be destroying corn: 'Fly, beetle; the ravenous wolf pursues you.'

Similar charms and exorcisms as well as many others have been used by professional vermin-killers in various parts of Europe, especially France, although by no means unknown in England. St Gertrude of Nivelles (626–59) was long regarded as the patroness of rat-catchers, and it was considered sufficient to murmur her name and bid the rats depart for that to happen. At other exorcisms or banishments of rats it was considered essential to adjure the rats – and in particular the great king of the rats – to 'remember' St Gertrude.

In the crypt of the saint's church at Nivelles there is a well whose water was long sought by people from far and wide, since, sprinkled in the house or over the fields or in the barns, it was thought to drive away all rats and mice. Earth from the tomb of St Ulric at Augsburg was said to have the same effect. Interestingly enough, it was often considered necessary to name a place to which the expelled rats could retreat and to take care that, if there was any running water between, a bridge was available over which they might pass.

Other spells and charms and exorcisms used less potent ingredients, and a reputedly powerful conjuration for getting rid of hares and rabbits involved the use of salt and rabbits' hair mixed together on a plate. At sunrise the operator or exorcist would proceed to the place where the charm was to be worked and, bare-headed and kneeling, he would 'cross' the mixture and distribute portions into various holes, murmuring an incantation that sometimes invoked the names of 'Heliot and Valiot Rouvayet' – whoever they may be, they were regarded as invaluable in keeping rabbits and hares at bay. The use of those names even extended to the personal protection of the exorcist, for if he should chance to encounter a hare on his way home, a most unlucky encounter in normal circumstances, the charm would protect him and he would come to no harm.

The ceremonies attending the exorcism of animals were

sometimes accompanied by a loud clashing of musical instruments. The *Confessions* of St Patrick (*c*.385–*c*.461) are considered to be documents of 'unquestioned authenticity', and he reveals that when he was unable to drive away a cloud of bats (which had been taken for demons) with the most formidable interdicts and powerful formulas for exorcism, he resorted to a deafening clashing of cymbals and, perhaps understandably, this drove the bats away in a great fright!

Undoubtedly the greatest of the numerous miracles ascribed to St Patrick is the driving out of Ireland all venomous reptiles and rendering the Irish soil for ever so obnoxious to the serpent race that they instantaneously die on touching it. Colgan (quoted by William Jones FSA in his *Credulities Past and Present*, 1880) seriously relates that St Patrick accomplished this unique and truly remarkable feat by beating a drum '… which he struck with such fervour that he knocked a hole in it, thereby endangering the success of the miracle'; but an angel appeared and mended the drum, and the patched instrument was long exhibited in Ireland as a holy relic.

The Rev. Alban Butler, however, in his *Life of St Patrick*, states that this particular 'benediction' employed the use of the saint's 'staff' (called 'the Staff of Jesus') which was preserved and venerated in Dublin. Snakes are similarly supposed to shun the island of Malta through the intercession of St Paul after he had been bitten on that island by a viper.

The Jesuit Pedro A. Ribadeneira (1527–1611) refers to the 'most famous' miracle of St Patrick, who '… did so free Ireland of all venomous beasts, that none ever since live or breathe there; and that even the very wood has a virtue against poison, so that it is reported of King's College, Cambridge, that being built of Irish wood, no spider doth ever come near it.'

There was from time immemorial the belief that rats could be extirpated by cursing them in rhyme. Reginald Scot, in his *Discoverie of Witchcraft* (1584), states that the Irish thought they could rhyme any beast to death, but in practice the idea was generally restricted to the rat. It is interesting to recall the legend of the Pied Piper of Hamelin, made famous by Robert Browning, and the tradition that the rats tumbled over themselves in their thousands to follow the piper's tune. On a prosaic note it has to be said that one version of the story has the Pied Piper luring the rats with a pocketful of valerian – rats and cats being much attracted to this plant, which is also known as All-heal.

Shakespeare refers to the rhyming belief or practice in *As You Like It*, where he has Rosalind say: 'I never was so berhymed since Pythagoras's time that I was an Irish rat, which I can hardly remember.'

Excommunication of animals is by no means unknown – or rather services of excommunication administered against animals is not unknown. In North America, towards the end of the seventeenth century, the Baron de la Hontan relates that the number of doves was so great in Montreal that the bishop was 'obliged' to excommunicate them several times, on account of the damage they had done.

In Brazil ants were excommunicated. At the beginning of the eighteenth century, the monks at the monastery of St Anthony brought an action at law against these insects, to obtain their removal. Manoel Bernardes in his *Nova Floresta* (Lisbon, 1706) gives an interesting account of this singular process, of which the following is an abbreviated translation:

> This extraordinary process took place between the friars of the province of Pietade, in Maranhao, and the ants of that territory. According to the monks numerous ants, which were very large and destructive, were extending their subterranean territory and to fill their store-houses had so undermined the cellars of the friars, in penetrating under their foundations, that the whole building was insecure. In addition the ants stole the grain that was laid up for the daily consumption of the convent and as the multitude of ants indefatigably worked day and night, the friars suffered and tried to stop the progress of the ants, but without success, their numbers being so great.
>
> As a last resource a friar recommended that an action should be brought against the ants before the tribunal of Divine Providence, and he named certain lawyers who should plead for and against them, and suggested that their bishop should be the judge to determine the case.
>
> This suggestion was acted upon and the trial commenced, the lawyer for the friars stating the complaint against the ants; and as it was contested by the legal representative of the ants, he proceeded to state that as the friars, conformably to the statues of their order, lived on the contributions they collected with great difficulty from the inhabitants of their district, and that the ants, who were looked upon as unholy, and for that reason were held in abhorrence, even by St Francis, continuously robbed them, and not only acted as thieves but seemed determined to expel the friars from their convent and ruin it.
>
> In consequence, the friars maintained, the ants were bound to

state their motives for their actions; or if not, they ought all to die of some pestilence, or be drowned by some inundation, or, at the very least, they should be exterminated for ever from the district.

The lawyer for the ants alleged in their defence that, having received from the creator the gift of life, they had a perfect right to preserve it by all the means that had been granted to them; that in the practice and execution of these measures they gave to men the example of virtues with which they had been endowed: prudence, in thinking of the future; diligence, in gathering in this life a recompense for the future; charity, in aiding each other when the duty was too heavy for their strength; and religion and piety, in burying their dead. They, or rather their lawyer, also maintained that the labour they had in working was much more severe than that which the plaintiffs could possibly appreciate, for the burden was often greater than their body, but their courage was superior to their strength.

While admitting that there were friars more noble and more worthy, yet before God *they* were only like ants, and the advantage of reason scarcely compensated their sin in having offended the Creator of all this in not observing the laws of reason as well as showing regard to creators of nature. By their present action the friars had rendered themselves unworthy of being served and succoured by any creature; for they had committed a greater crime in acting in so many ways against the glory of God, than the ants had done in taking their flour.

Also, it was maintained, the ants (the defendants) were in possession of the ground before the friars had established themselves in the place, and, in consequence, they ought not to be expelled; and they would appeal against this violence to the tribunal of their Divine Creator, who made the smallest as well as the greatest, and had assigned to every one a guardian angel. In conclusion it was pointed out that the plaintiffs defended their house and their flour by human means which they (the ants) could not contest, but, it was averred, the defendants would continue their mode of living, as the earth, and all it contained, belonged to God, and not to the plaintiffs.

This reply occasioned much discussion and the lawyer for the friars felt himself constrained to admit that the debate had proved the ants to have some right on their side. So the judge, after a careful perusal of the evidence, and due consideration, decreed that the friars should select a field in their neighbourhood where the ants should be left in possession. The change of dwelling and removal was to take place immediately, under pain of excommunication.

This sentence delivered and by order of the judge, a friar went to deliver it to the ants, reading it in a loud voice before the openings of the ant-hills; and marvellous was the effect for immediately millions of ants came out, forming themselves in long and dense columns, and proceeded direct to the field assigned to them, abandoning their former dwellings; while the friars, released from their insupportable oppressors, returned thanks to God for such a manifestation of His power and providence.

Manoel Bernardes adds that this sentence was pronounced on 17 January 1713 and that he had seen the full accounts of the lawsuit in the monastery of St Anthony, where they are preserved.

Nor is this by any manner of means the only instance of such 'exorcism' and threat of excommunication. In the eighteenth century in Peru termites, or white ants, which had invaded a library and had damaged and partially destroyed a great number of books, had an excommunication pronounced against them. The French navigator Comte de La Perouse (1741–88) describes in his *Voyages*, collected into four volumes and published posthumously in 1797, how he and his men found '... millions of cockroaches in the bread-room, so that the holy father who officiated as chaplain was obliged to recourse to exorcisms more than once'.

There have been excommunications against swallows – for defiling the head of Ekbert, Bishop of Trèves, when he was performing mass at the altar of St Peter's Church in Rome; against sparrows who similarly misbehaved themselves on worshippers in another church in another country; and William, Abbot of St Theodoric, wrote a *Life of St Bernard* (1090–1153) in which he reveals that one day while the saint was preaching in the church of Foigny, a 'prodigious number of flies entering, troubled his hearers' by their buzzing and aimless flights, whereupon the saint excommunicated them '... and the next day all the flies were found dead'. Their bodies covered the church floor and pavement, and the story of the miracle spread far and wide, resulting in 'curing the flies' becoming a byword in the area.

The Church of Rome favoured the period between the feast of Easter and Ascension Day for the exorcizing of rats, caterpillars, flies and other animals, and in 1880, William Johes FSA, cited the following account written by a priest engaged in such a service:

> I went during the course of my residence at Bologna in Italy to exorcize the insects in that country, accompanied by a curate, who was a droll fellow, and laughed at the credulity of the people while he pocketed their money. He did not tie himself down to the ritual or form prescribed by the Church, but made his own comments upon everything: sometimes he spoke to the ants, sometimes to the

grasshoppers; at other times to the rats, lizards or worms. He banished them all, one after another, to the several countries he designed as the places of their exile. The moles he ordered to travel to the antarctic pole; he had scarcely pronounced the sentence when a mole came forth from under its little hillock, whereupon the curate cried out, 'Courage, my friend; look, there is one of them ready to begin its march!' But the mole, it seems, had no inclination for the journey, and therefore ran into a hole not far distant. One of the peasants followed it, and kneeling down peeped into the hole, and turning to the curate, said, very innocently, 'Pray, sir, is this the antarctic pole?' We could not forebear laughing; but as this was diametrically opposite to that gravity which it was necessary to assume upon these occasions, we begged him to desist.

Few authentic historical articles associated with exorcism exist today, especially anything associated with the exorcism of animals, but many years ago, when we lived at Strawberry Hill, Twickenham, we obtained special permission to visit Strawberry Hill itself, the Gothic-style mansion in the form of a castle that Horace Walpole built between 1750 and 1776, and there heard for the first time about a large silver bell that had once been one of the treasures of the place.

This curious object, my wife and I were told, was made by Benvenuto Cellini (1500–1571), the Italian artist who produced the famous bronze 'Perseus with the head of Medusa': one of the most typical and unforgettable monuments of the Italian Renaissance. Cellini had been apprenticed to a goldsmith and he made silver vessels of every description. This silver bell was among articles he made, we were told, for Pope Clement VII and was elaborately carved on the exterior with representations of serpents, flies, grasshoppers and other creatures. Its purpose was to serve in papal cursing of these animals when they, on occasion, became so troublesome as to warrant such castigation; it had also been used for exorcism of animals. My initial enquiries revealed that it had been dispersed by auction in 1842, and I then set about making enquiries in Britain and America to trace its present whereabouts.

When we lived at Strawberry Hill I had been in correspondence with Wilmarth Sheldon Lewis, the great American authority and collector of works and possessions of Horace Walpole, whose story *The Castle of Otranto* is a Gothic masterpiece of horror. W.S. Lewis had been delighted by our letterhead: 'Otranto', Walpole Road, Strawberry Hill, Twicken-

ham, which he told me would be preserved for all time in his
Walpole collection at Yale University!

So I wrote to Yale and also to St Mary's College, which is now
housed at Strawberry Hill, to establish in writing that they did
not have the bell. The Head of History at the College replied:
'We haven't, ourselves, got the bell, and, if it still exists, it could
well be at Yale. Are you aware that there were *two* auctions in
the nineteenth century, both of them called Great Sales? The
first one was in 1842 and the second in 1883. The catalogue for
these sales are available and an auctioneers' copy could well
have details of purchasers of the items in these sales. It might be
worth your while to enquire at the Victoria and Albert Museum
because there are a number of items from Walpole's collection in
their galleries.' I wrote at once to the Victoria and Albert
Museum.

I then had a reply from Yale, on paper headed The Lewis
Walpole Library, a Department of Yale University and from the
material that Marie Devine PhD, the librarian, kindly enclosed I
learned a lot about the bell. The first mention of the bell, it
seems, is in a letter to Sir Horace Mann, dated 14 February 1772,
where Horace Walpole says: 'Wish me joy; I have changed all
my Roman medals of great brass, some of which were very fine,
particularly a *medaglioncino* of Alexander Severus which is
unique, for the uniquest thing in the world, a silver bell for an
inkstand made by Benvenuto Cellini. It makes one believe all the
extravagant encomiums he bestows on himself – indeed so does
his Perseus. Well, *my* bell is in the finest taste, and is swarmed
by caterpillars, lizards, grasshoppers, flies, and masques, that
you would take it for one of the plagues of Egypt. They are all in
altissimo, nay, in out-*issimo* relievo, and yet almost invisible but
with a glass. Such foliage, such fruitage! ...'

In Walpole's own *Description of the Villa of Horace Walpole*
(Strawberry Hill, 1774) he again describes the bell: 'A most
beautiful silver bell, made for a pope by Benvenuto Cellini. It is
covered all over in the highest relievo with antique masks, flies,
grasshoppers, and other insects; the virgin and boy-angels at
top, a wreath of leaves at bottom. Nothing can exceed the taste
of the whole design, or the delicate and natural representation
of the insects: the wonderful execution makes almost every
thing credible that He says of himself in his Life. It came out of
the collection of the marquis Leonati at Palma, and was bought

by the marquis of Rockingham, who exchanged it with Mr Walpole for some very scarce Roman medals of great bronze ...' And in a letter published in John Pinkerton's *Walpoliana* (1799) Walpole says: 'One of the pieces in my collection which I most highly value, is the silver bell with which the popes used to curse the caterpillars; a ceremony I believe now abandoned. Lahontan, in his travels, mentions a like absurd custom in Canada, the solemn excommunication, by the bishop, of the turtle-doves, which greatly injured the plantations ... Cellini, the artist, was one of the most extraordinary men in an extraordinary age. His life, written by himself, is more amusing than any novel I know.'

Meanwhile I had a reply from Dr C. Wainwright, assistant keeper of the Department of Furniture and Interior Design at the Victoria and Albert Museum, who told me: 'The bell still survives. It is now in the collection of the department of Medieval and later Antiquities at the British Museum ... It is now known that it is not by Cellini but is actually German but of quite similar date.'

And so to the British Museum, where Mr Hugh Tait supplied me with a copy of his Waddesdon Bequest Catalogue with its marvellously detailed description of 'the so-called Cellini bell': 'Origin – Nuremberg; mid-16th century; no marks; attributed to Wenzel Jamnitzer (master 1534, died 1585). Measurements: H. 5.3 in; Diam. of rim 3.7 in; Weight 835 g. Condition: Excellent, although there are signs of alteration around the aperture in the handle.'

It transpires that the remarkable 'Cellini' bell is something of a mystery in more ways than one. It may have been meant to be purely ornamental, for a desk or table (which surely seems unlikely), or for 'some ecclesiastical purpose', and that purpose was, in all probability and in my opinion, for the cursing, excommunication and exorcism of animals.

In 1845 an ancient Irish amulet was found at Timeoleage in County Cork. It was in the form of a large caterpillar and made of silver. It was hollow and had the back and sides coated with pieces of glass and composition of various colours, chiefly yellows, with a streak of dark blue on either side, and red along the back. The length was about 4½ inches overall, and it was about two inches in circumference. This amulet is an exact imitation, in size, colour and appearance, of the caterpillar called by country people the murrain, It is in fact the caterpillar of the elephant hawkmoth, and eating the larva of this moth, and possibly the caterpillar too, was said to cause murrain – a contagious and malignant cattle fever. Murrain was the fifth plague visited upon the Egyptians (Exodus 9:3). Understandably this insect was held in great dread by the farming community, and it seems likely that this Irish jewel was used as an amulet, being hired out to the farmers for the purpose of curing or exorcizing the murrain.

A mild form of exorcism was sometimes all that was necessary, and we have an instance of such activity on the part of St Ailbhe. It seems that when large flocks of birds destroyed the corn in the neighbourhood and could not be dispersed, the saint went and delivered an oration to them on the unreasonableness of their conduct, and '... forthwith, penitent and ashamed, they soared into the air, and went away.'

There is a story too concerning St Pol de Léon, a saint of Brittany, that when still a boy he gave an indication of his future life as a saint. The fields of the monastery in which he was a student were ravaged by such a number of birds that the whole crop of corn was in danger of being lost. St Pol, young as he was, summoned the sacrilegious birds to appear before the principal of the monastery, St Hydultus, to receive the correction they deserved. The birds, obedient to the summons, accordingly presented themselves in a body at the appointed time but St Hydultus, 'being of a humane disposition', only gave them a reproof and admonition and then let them go – even giving them a benediction at their departure! The grateful birds, we are told, never again touched the corn of the monastery.

Englishmen were no less keen to preserve their corn, and Lambarde in his *Perambulation of Kent* (written in 1570) refers to the image of St Edith at Kemsing where the corn did not suffer damage by wind, mildew, brand-ear or other injuries due to the intervention of the power of St Edith – who is regarded as the representative of Robigus, or Robigo, a Latin deity whose special duties included the protection of cornfields from blight and other dangers.

Here there was a form of sacrifice: the farmer who wished to screen his crops from evil influences took a few pecks of corn to the priest, who, after putting by the chief part for his own use, took a single handful of the grain, sprinkled it with holy water and 'by mumbling of a fewe wordes of conjuration' dedicated it to St Edith. He then gave it back to the farmer, who departed in the full belief that by his mixing the hallowed handful with his seed-corn, the coming crop would be insured against all calamities.

For years a somewhat similar cleansing ceremony was performed by girls in many parts of Russia. On the first day of September they would make small coffins of turnips and other vegetables, enclose flies and other insects in them and then bury them with a great show of mourning.

An even stranger custom was the explusion of tarakans, a kind of cockroach, which took place on the eve of St Philip's Day. A thread would be fastened to one of these large insects, and all the inmates of the affected cottage, with closed lips, would unite in dragging it out of doors. While the expulsion was going on, one of the women of the family would stand with dishevelled hair at a window, and when the cockroach was on the threshold, she would knock and ask what food the occupants had most enjoyed. 'Beef,' the occupant of the cottage would reply. 'And the tarakan, what?' she would then ask. 'The tarakan on tarakans,' came the answer. If the ceremony was properly performed, it was thought that the tarakans were prevented from ever returning to the cottage. On the other hand, there were always those who deemed such acts of expulsion wrong, considering that the presence of such insects also brought blessings.

On certain holy days it was considered necessary to sprinkle the flocks and herds with holy water, for at the time there were thought to be in Russia wolves in the shape of black dogs, cats that sucked cows, mares and ewes and female animals that slaughtered their male companions.

An ancient and possibly druidic custom was at one time prevalent in Scotland when a contagious disease 'entered among cattle'. A fire in the house would be extinguished and then relit by rubbing a piece of dry wood upon another, and branches of the evergreen juniper would be set alight and bunches would be taken to the stalls of the cattle, for it was believed that the smoke would purify the air. They also boiled juniper in water which they then sprinkled upon the cattle; this done, the fires in the house would be extinguished and lighted again without the juniper.

The sun festival was called Beltane or Beltein, and the fires that were lit were called Baal fires: ceremonies which preserved the flocks and destroyed harmful animals. An old volume by Pennant (1726–98) on his *Tour of Scotland* describes the festival in some detail:

> On the first of May, the herdsmen of every village held their Beltein, a rural sacrifice. They cut a square of trench in the ground, leaving the turf in the middle; on that they made a fire of wood, on which they dress a large caudle of eggs, butter, oatmeal, and milk, and bring, besides the ingredients of the caudle, plenty of beer and whiskey; for each of the company must contribute something. The rites begin with spilling some of the caudle on the ground, by way of libation; on that, every one takes a cake of oatmeal, upon which are raised nine square knobs, each dedicated to some particular being, the supposed preserver of their flocks, or to some particular animal, the destroyer of them; each person then turns his face to the fire, breaks off a knob, and flinging it over his shoulder, says: 'This I give to thee! Preserve thou my horses! This to thee, preserve thou my sheep!'
>
> After that they use the same ceremony to the noxious animals: 'This I give to thee, oh Fox! spare thou my lambs! This to thee, oh hooded Crow! This to thee, oh Eagle!' When the ceremony is over, they dine on the caudle, and after the feast is finished, what is left is hid by two persons deputed for the purpose; but on the next Sunday they reassemble, and finish the relics of the first entertainment.

Reverting to Russia, there used to be a curious custom, almost an exorcism, for driving off an epidemic. The female inhabitants of the village would heap up two piles of rubbish at midday, one at each end of the village, and at midnight they would set them both alight. To one of these bonfires the girls, dressed in white, would drag a plough, one of their number following the rest and carrying a holy picture. A black cock would be taken to the other bonfire by older women and carried three times round the flames. Then one of the women would seize the bird and run with it to the other end of the village, the rest following and shouting words and phrases such as 'Disappear, perish, black disease …' When the leading woman reached the burning fire at the other end of the village, she would fling the bird into the fire. Such a sacrifice was regarded as infallible in driving off an epidemic.

There is a famous healing talisman which Sir Walter Scott acknowledged to have suggested to him the title for his book *The Talisman*; this is the Lee Penny, a heart-shaped pebble of cornelian agate set in a silver coin. It has long had the reputation of being unrivalled in combating illness in cattle and occasionally in man.

Legend has it that Robert the Bruce, King of Scotland, wanted his heart to be taken to the Holy Land after his death, and in 1329 Lord James of Douglas and Simon Locard of Lee set out on this mission. In Spain they were drawn into battle with the Moors, and when Douglas was killed, Locard, who now commanded the party, turned homeward with Bruce's heart, which was eventually buried in the Abbey of Dunfermline.

Locard had taken prisoner a Moorish chieftain, and when the aged mother of this man came to the Scottish camp to redeem her son for an agreed amount, Locard noticed a curious silver coin among the possessions of the old lady and he demanded that it be added to the ransom. Somewhat unwillingly the woman consented and explained to Simon Locard the stone's power in healing animals and the mode in which it could be put to use. So the Lee Penny came into the hands of the Locard or Lockhart family, where it still resides.

The stone was supposed to cure 'all diseases in cattle and the bite of a mad dog both in man and beast'. To work, the stone had to be dipped three times in water and swirled round once, the water then being given to the diseased cattle to drink or, in the case of a dog bite, applied as a lotion to the wound. No words should be used when the stone was dipped and no money taken for the use of the Lee Penny.

The talisman is said to have been frequently employed with considerable success for 600 years, and there are many recorded instances of its potency. Of particular interest is a remarkable case performed about 1750 on Lady Baird of Sauchton near Edinburgh. She had the misfortune to be bitten by a mad dog and contracted hydrophobia. At length her husband, Sir Robert Baird, in an agony of despair, remembered the famous Lee Penny and stories of its efficacy in cases of bites by mad dogs. He sent an urgent message requesting the loan of the talisman. The Penny was sent to Sir Robert, an unusual favour, since it was not normally allowed out of the house, and Lady Baird retained it for several weeks, drinking and bathing and using as a lotion on the wound the water in which the talisman had been dipped. In due course she made a full recovery; the Lee Penny was returned to its owners, and they were entertained to a sumptuous meal by the Bairds.

The last recorded occurrence when the Penny is said to have been used was more than seventy years ago. The late Sir Simon Lockhart was entertaining a shooting party at his seat, Lee, and among the guests was a relative of the then Lord Hamilton of Dalzell. At luncheon on the moors it was discovered that no bottle-opener had been brought along, and Sir Simon tried to use a pocket-knife while Lord Hamilton's relative held the bottle. Unfortunately the knife slipped and Sir Simon's guest had a badly cut hand. The wound was roughly dressed but the wound was quite deep, and at dinner the man complained that he could not stop the bleeding. Sir Simon was much concerned and took the man aside and led him into his library. There he opened a safe and brought out the Lee Penny, which he placed in a basin of water. He then had his friend plunge his hand into the water, bandaged as it was, and urged him to keep it there for some little time. After a while the bleeding stopped, and next morning, according to a contemporary report, the wound was completely healed, except for a small dry scar in the centre.

Before leaving the subject of exorcism and animals, let us take a look at the recent exorcism of a cat. In the book about her cat, *Rogan*, Jane Conyngham Bailey writes about the many people in all parts of the country who had seemingly benefited from Rogan's 'teaching and healing'. It is a quite remarkable story. When she and Rogan moved to East Anglia, Mrs Bailey felt that she might unwittingly have offended some people who formed part of a large coven of witches in that part of the world, with the result that her house became 'haunted'. The place was exorcized by a retired vicar, but not before Mrs Bailey became convinced that the 'visitations' were being directed at Rogan, culminating in his suffering a curious kind of lockjaw. The cat was examined by a veterinary surgeon who found Rogan was perfectly able to open his mouth to yawn or lick his fur but as soon as he attempted to eat food his jaws locked and became immovable. Within days he was half his usual weight.

Utterly convinced by now – since there appeared to be nothing physically wrong with the cat and since the veterinary surgeon could suggest no treatment – that 'evil agencies' were attempting to kill the cat, Mrs Bailey went back to see the priest who had exorcized her house. He too was sure that Rogan was cursed, and he asked Mrs Bailey to bring the cat to his house, where he would exorcize him.

During the exorcism Rogan 'struggled and shook, cursed and spat, and severely scratched the priest's hands', eventually escaping to hide under a chair. However, once home again, Rogan was able to eat a little food. Three days later he was exorcized again, and this time Rogan's reactions were '… much less violent and without a doubt', says Mrs Bailey, 'he was freed of whatever evil had been visited upon him'. Mrs Bailey bought a silver crucifix, and this Rogan wore round his neck for the rest of his life.

It is necessary to read Mrs Bailey's book in full to appreciate the whole fascinating story but it cannot but be interesting to note that a service of exorcism can apparently affect some animals as well as some human beings.

4   Exorcism and Possession

Demons and evil spirits, hovering on the fringes of the human mind, have been blamed for every conceivable crime, including murder. Both the 1978 chainsaw murderer and the Yorkshire Ripper, Peter Sutcliffe, who murdered thirteen women between 1975 and 1980, claimed that voices urged them to accomplish their atrocities, and they were by no means the only mass murderers to make such a claim.

One American 'expert on demonology' claims he was burned by invisible forms and sliced and cut; marks and symbols were, he claims, gouged on his body and he was thrown 'across the room like a toy ...' In another case car tyres were slashed, bottles containing a variety of substances were 'picked up by invisible hands' and carried along and then emptied elsewhere. The house and the occupants in the latter case were examined by a Roman Catholic priest who sprinkled holy water and commanded the 'unclean spirit' to depart. Afterwards the whole family said they saw a strange white figure appear, and they all experienced a smell of rotting flesh. 'Begone,' commanded the priest, and the figure vanished, leaving 'a pink outline' on the carpet.

Can such experiences be explained by the term 'possession'?[1] Possession is generally considered to be a state in which gods, spirits, devils or a personality other than that of the individual concerned takes charge of his or her body and mind; such a person is then considered to be possessed. Possession, and in particular demonic possession, is a phenomenon as old as man himself, and there is an enormous literature on the subject of gods, demons and various discarnate entities allegedly entering the human body and taking control of the personality.

While possession by a god or holy spirit may be regarded as a high and valuable experience, it would seem that, conversely, possession by an evil spirit or a bad personality can be damaging and highly dangerous. Possession has been variously described as ecstasy, hysteria, enthusiasm and mania; and perhaps partly explained by the fact that a characteristic of possession is always a feeling of giddiness – a word derived from *gidig* in Middle English, which meant 'to be possessed by a god'.

States of possession have been induced from earliest times, during Dionysian celebrations, through medieval Europe to the present-day preoccupation with music, dancing, physical exercise, alcohol, drugs and sex. Some states of possession, both induced and spontaneous, include physical changes: the person becomes changed facially, and witnesses see evil features appear; the body may become wasted, the stomach distended; the complexion pales and there may be vomiting and foul breath. Internal discomforts have also been experienced, described by the victims as like an animal eating away at the entrails. Often the subject will experience sudden body blows which leave marks; there may be convulsions, fainting fits and catatonic withdrawal and posturing; the voice may become gruff and the language obscene or blasphemous; and, very often, there is a feeling of extreme coldness in the vicinity of the affected person.

Psychologists believe that cases of possession have nothing to do with spirits of any kind but that the answer lies in greatly increased brain activity, often the result of emotional excitement or upheaval; while the student of the paranormal points to the relative ease with which apparent possession is achieved, the spontaneous appearance of possession in many diverse individuals, and the evidence of anthropologists whose researches show that states of possession are achieved in primitive societies in ways that vary from rhythmic drumming to excessive sexual excitation. It seems likely that ninety-nine per cent of cases of possession have an emotional basis.

In 1975 the present writer was approached by a correspondent who claimed that his mind and body were being invaded by 'earthbound spirits'. He found himself behaving in a way completely foreign to his usual self, and among other disturbing symptoms he suddenly developed masochistic tendencies which resulted in his attempting to mutilate himself.

After his receiving 'spiritual healing', the masochism receded into the background, but 'increasingly' he heard threatening voices all around him, accompanied by 'very unpleasant sensations' both within and outside his body. Soon he began to glimpse 'spirit forms', and he recognized two of them as long-deceased people he had known. Then he felt that he was being attacked from inside his body, and at length he went to see a psychologist, then a psychiatrist and clergymen of various denominations, but the sensations continued and in fact increased to the point at which he found himself constantly being harassed and harangued by threatened voices, preventing him from sleeping and urging him to mutilate himself.

I contacted my friend Dr William Sargant, at that time head of the Department of Psychological Medicine at St Thomas's Hospital. From his address in Harley Street he told me he thought the man was psychologically ill and should go and see his local psychiatrist again. He added that he did not believe that evil spirits existed – although of course there was plenty of evil in the world.

When this course of action had no effect, I contacted the leading exorcist of the day, the Rev. Dr Robert Petitpierre, and he said he would gladly do what he could to help in what sounded like 'a rather sticky case'. He recommended a doctor and a psychiatrist, 'because there was clearly a deep-seated complex and problem' to be overcome. Eventually he talked to the man, conducted a service of exorcism and achieved a complete cure – or so I was informed.

Some twenty years ago, I learned when visiting the Eternal City that a four-day battle had taken place between a parish priest in Rome and eight demons; a battle that had also ended in complete victory for the Church. For weeks, I was told, the inhabitants of a small village in north Italy considered a 16-year-old peasant's daughter, Celestina Taddeo, to be a girl 'possessed'. Eight different voices, all deep and masculine, issued from her lips and, not dreaming they could be the voices of eight devils, the girl's mother took her daughter to see a doctor. To her surprise, he said he could do nothing.

The girl began to speak in a language that neither her mother nor anyone else could comprehend or understand, until Latin scholars pronounced that it was grammatically correct ancient Latin, although some of the words and phrases were surprising and questionable, coming from the mouth of a young lady.

Then Signora Taddeo took her daughter to a well-known

specialist in exorcism, Father Gennaro Laurora, and he declared that the girl was possessed by eight devils which he proceeded to name: Ashtaroth, Beelzebub, Samuel, Piton, Asmodeus, Belial, Satan and Lucifer.

He set to work at once to cast out the talkative demons, and the first to 'come forth' was Ashtaroth, 'who nevertheless put up quite a fight, swearing horribly' as he succumbed to the power of the exorcist. Ordered by the priest to leave the girl in peace and return to Hell, Ashtaroth fled, leaving his victim writhing unconscious on the church floor.

As soon as Celestina regained consciousness, she was heard to be speaking on behalf of Beelzebub, whose Latin was even more improper than that of Ashtaroth! Beelzebub too put up a long fight, but finally he was 'downed' by Don Gennaro Laurora, 'who sent him packing to the infernal regions'.

Celestina's mother felt that by this time her daughter was cured, and in any case she had had enough for one day, so she took her daughter home. But soon other devils took possession of her, and her mother contacted the exorcist and took the girl back to him, and the exorcisms started again.

Each day the exorcist worked on long and painful sessions, during which the girl fainted several times. The ritual had to be postponed and, being interrupted, had to be begun all over again. But eventually six other devils were cast out in turn, and finally, four days after the first visit to the exorcist, the priest tackled the two toughest devils, Satan and Lucifer.

This pair tried every possible trick they knew, I was assured, reciting the words ahead of the priest and roaring with infernal laughter during the solemn ceremony; but finally, when Don Gennaro himself was almost totally exhausted, two empty benches in the church flew up into the air by themselves and then crashed down – the signal, it was thought, that Lucifer himself had been cast out.

Celestina returned home and, according to my informant in Rome, never again spoke in ancient Latin or indeed spoke at all except in her own sweet Italian voice. It was, it seems, a remarkable and resounding success for the Italian exorcist; a positive success over possession.

I am indebted to Joseph H. Crehan SJ for drawing my attention to a fascinating document that had been 'stumbled upon' by Herbert Thurston SJ. It appears as an appendix to an edition of the *Rituale Romanum*, published with the full authorization of the Council of the Inquisition, at the Royal Printing Office, Madrid, in 1631, and concerns a house that was 'possessed', rather than a person.

The document was headed 'Exorcism of a House Troubled by an Evil Spirit', and the priest was directed to wear surplice and stole and to begin with the words, 'In the name of the Father and of the Son and of the Holy Ghost, Amen,' making at the same time a triple sign of the cross. The priest or priests endeavouring to cast out the devils possessing the haunted house were to recite the first five of the Gradual Psalms (Psalms 119–123) while every part of the house was visited and sprinkled with holy water; the round ended with a few versicles as an introduction to an appropriate prayer. Then the second set of five Gradual Psalms was to be recited while the officiating priest and his assistants again visited every part of the house, sprinkling holy water and ending with a different prayer. Then for the third and last time the whole house was to be sprinkled, while the five remaining Gradual Psalms were recited, ending with yet another prayer.

After this there were to be read the extracts from the Gospels concerning Zacchaeus, the publican, which are read in the mass for the dedication of a church and were thought to be especially appropriate in releasing a house from being possessed. Incense was then to be put into the thurible, and the whole house incensed, and after further prayers the priests present would all give their blessings, sprinkling holy water and then departing. For the exorcism of a particular demon, it was stated, special faculties must be granted if the possessed was a person but this was not necessary when the possession had affected a place and not a particular person. On the other hand, it was stressed, no ceremonial of this liturgical character ought to be employed by private initiative or without episcopal sanction.

In 1976 the General Assembly laid down guidelines for the Church of Scotland in dealing with cases of apparent possession by demons and detailed what procedures were allowable in this 'psychic minefield', in both a public and a private pastoral sense.

Presenting this report on exorcism, the Rev. Stewart Lamont, who visited my home in 1978 when we talked at length about ghosts and haunted houses and exorcism, said: 'There is little doubt that the ceremonial of exorcism appeals to a small minority of clergymen who find it exciting and feel they are endowed with magic powers. Others may undertake it with sincere intentions, but misguided judgement. We do not pretend that cases of "possession" are very common – even the Anglican clergymen who exorcize persons (as opposed to places) say that most of their clients require a doctor and not exorcism.'

Mr Lamont went on to say that there was always the danger of mistaking symptoms of physical or mental disorder as being caused by demons. Apart from the possibility of worsening the patient's conditions, this could only serve to undo much progress that had been made during the past thirty years in the understanding of psychiatric illness.

Mr Lamont said it had to be remembered that most of the people exhibiting symptoms of 'possession' were among the neurotic and emotionally unstable and the mentally ill. 'Demons are not contagious,' he said. 'They are not caught in cinemas showing horror films, or in dark cupboards, they do not spread epidemics, but panic can, and panic can carry symptoms without the disease, just as the obsessive world of the medieval church found witches in every village.'

Finally Mr Lamont added: 'Western medical science may not know all the answers. But it is all that we have, and if we ignore it in favour of the crass superstition and return to exorcistic ceremonies, then we risk the contempt of the medical profession. That is why we recommend the reference to a physician be mandatory in cases of so-called "possession".'

Exorcism of the apparently possessed does vary considerably. There is the lay exorcist who believes, for example, that three people together who have been baptized are all-powerful against the powers of evil; and there are legends of prevention and cure for cases of possession and similar manifestations that echo down the centuries: that a cross erected at the scene of a fatal accident will prevent the ghost's walking and anyone's becoming possessed by the spirit of someone killed there; that ghostly victims of an assassin will walk or will possess someone's body until the assassin meets his end; that a ghost will never walk if the shoes a person wore when they died are buried with them, nor will their spirit have the power to possess anyone.

Sometimes, as we shall see, a layman's prayers do seem to be sufficient to lay a ghost or release a possessed person; sometimes, it seems, the sign of the cross will do the same thing, and often common-sense works wonders.

A chapel on the Continent was long haunted by the ghost of a priest who celebrated a ghostly Mass there once a year. After a courageous lay exorcist attended one of the spectral services and gave the responses as the ceremony proceeded, the ghostly sights and sounds ceased: seemingly this was what that particular ghost had been waiting for; the lay exorcist regarded the chapel as being possessed, he acted as he saw right in cases of possession, and it seems to have worked.

The French writer Monsignor L. Cristiani has pointed out in his book *Satan and the Modern World* that many cases of apparent possession occur today and are dealt with exactly as they were centuries ago, by exorcism. In particular Monsignor Cristiani gives a detailed account of how a devil was driven out of a woman in 1954.

It is a dramatic and at times quite terrifying statement, told mostly in dialogue, of a duel between the priest and the demon, speaking through the possessed woman. The demon protests, mocks, lies and blasphemes, seeking to distract the priest and cause him to give up his attempts at exorcism. However, the priest remains adamant, and he sprinkles the woman with holy water, touches her with a crucifix and with his stole, and recites prayers and litanies – causing the demon great pain and distress. This exorcism ceremony continued over a period of many months but was eventually successful.

It has been suggested – with some degree of accuracy, it must be admitted – that a literal and anthropomorphic belief in the Devil may no longer be possible and that exorcism succeeds (in cases where it *does* succeed) in the somewhat puzzling way in which various forms of psychoanalysis and psychotherapy succeed: namely that for certain individuals religious exorcism seems to be the right way of approaching and curing (or relieving) mental disturbance. It has to be said, in passing, that accounts of dialogues between psychiatrists and schizophrenics show a marked similarity to dialogues between would-be exorcists and those who appear to be possessed by devils.

During the course of research for this volume, I approached Canon Dominic Walker OGS, who is regarded as a long-standing and current expert in religious exorcisms, and he told me: 'Although I have spent about ten years being involved in this kind of ministry, only on two occasions have I carried out the rite of exorcism with what would be traditionally described as a major exorcism rite. On many occasions I have prayed for people to be delivered from evil or temptation, although I suspect that you are more interested in exorcism as a means of dealing with possession rather than obsession (or infestation as it is sometimes known).

'I have to admit to being very sceptical about whether or not it is possible for someone to be possessed. This springs from my lack of belief in a personal devil and although I am happy to use such language as "the demonic", "the devil" and "evil spirits", I understand them as being an unintegrated part of the human condition which may be discerned symbolically; I do not understand such terminology as indicating belief in objective non-human entities.'

I had approached Canon Dominic Walker looking for some detailed examples of exorcisms and possibly some photographs; but of course I quite understood when the canon said: 'The difficulty that every priest faces when receiving a request such as yours is that we are bound by a very strict code of confidentiality, and I would certainly not be willing to put you in touch with anyone to whom I have ministered, and I am not able to provide photographs or detailed case histories.' I am, however, very grateful to Canon Walker for his interest and valuable comments and for allowing me to quote him.

A few years ago I took part in a four-hour television programme in Madrid with contributors from Spain, Germany and Italy as well as Britain. The whole thing was translated instantaneously, so that everyone could take part. The contributor and representative from Spain was Julio Caro Baroja, an acknowledged expert on witchcraft – the programme was devoted to ghosts and the paranormal in general – and before, during and after the live broadcast he had some interesting points to make about possession.

In the case of the nuns in the convent of St Placidus in Madrid (contemporary with the notorious Loudun affair of 1634, curiously enough), Baroja told me there are three versions of the story: 1. that of the inquisitors, which led to the condemnation of several nuns, together with their spiritual director; 2. the popular version; and 3. the version of Doña Teresa Valle de la

Cerda, mother superior in the convent, who after being condemned asked for her case to be reviewed, since she had acted out of pure obedience, and later she was granted complete absolution by the Inquisition.

According to the first version, the Benedictine father confessor of the nuns, Fray Francisco García Calderón, was a heretic, a lascivious and dominating personality who seriously harmed the women in his charge – they were possessed by the Devil after being seduced by their confessor. The case was investigated by inquisitors who were predisposed to condemn, and the father confessor was found guilty on serious suspicion of heresy, while the nuns were punished in various minor ways. But in fact the sentence against the friar was highly irregular, since it was based largely on charges which were probably false, making him out to be a repository of all kinds of heresy and ambition. (In 1638 King Philip IV of Spain is supposed to have been in love with a nun of the same convent, which had certainly acquired a bad reputation.)

The popular version of the story, which is later in date, describes the convent's patron, Don Jerónimo de Villanueva, as a sorcerer, claiming that he allowed all kinds of irregularities to go on; this version, Baroja was careful to point out to me, confuses the 'possession' part of the affair with a later case in which Philip IV and the Conde-Duque de Olivares were involved. It states that, while the King made love to a nun, the Conde-Duque and Don Jerónimo, the chief notary of Aragon, performed sacrilegious rites. Finally Doña Teresa Valle de la Cerda, when she asked for the sentence on the convent she had founded to be quashed, did not hesitate to admit that she had been possessed by a devil called Peregrine and that some twenty-five other nuns were also possessed by devils; she made no reference to sorcery at all.

To my mind, this case, perhaps more than any, clearly illustrates the considerable difficulty in ascertaining good and reliable accounts of possession, for Baroja had no doubt that in this, one of the better-known Spanish cases, there were one or two clergy who really were guilty parties, whilst the nuns who were implicated with them – possessed by the Devil, damned by popular opinion and even condemned by the authorities – seem to have been entirely blameless.

The late Gordon Wellesley, author of *Sex and the Occult*, told me about the method of religious exorcism witnessed by Dr Ainslie Meares, an eminent psychiatrist from Sydney, New South Wales – a practice detailed by the doctor in his volume *Strange Places and Simple Truths*:[2]

At Wollaso, some fifty or sixty miles from Addis Ababa, there is a man widely famed for his healing by exorcism of devils. The healer is a bishop of the Coptic Church. He is a big, imposing man with a beard, and a golden crucifix hangs on his chest over his black robes. It was a Sunday when I visited him, and he explained that he worked at exorcism on every day except Sunday which he kept free for a religious service. He explained in detail the exact procedure of ridding a patient of devils. His description was confirmed by a doctor, who was a frequent visitor to his healing sessions.

He showed me the place where he worked. It was a large ramshackle shed. There was a formal pulpit, and pews were arranged as in a church. At the back there was an old forty-four gallon drum which had been filled with water from a well in the yard. Attached to the forty-four gallon drum was a hand pump and a long length of garden hose. This led into an extension of the shed at the side of the pulpit. It is here that the exorcisms take place. Men and women strip to the waist. The bishop takes the nozzle of the hose in one hand and a large wooden cross in the other. A boy gets to work on the hand pump, and the bishop hoses the patient. At the same time he calls upon the devil to come out. The devil, in the voice of the patient, usually answers back, 'I won't come out. I won't come out'. Then, in the name of the Lord, the bishop commands the devil in a loud voice to leave his victim. Sometimes the devil uses the patient's voice to jeer at the bishop. Then force has to be used. As the devil speaks these profane words, the bishop gets to him by squirting the patient in the mouth. Sometimes he has to flog the devil out of the patient with heavy blows from his large wooden cross. If it seems that the devil is inhabiting the victim's head, he bangs the patient on the head with the cross. The devil is eventually defeated, and is anxious to leave the body of his victim. In the struggle of the devil to leave his body, the patient is frequently thrown to the floor, and often has a convulsive seizure. The bishop told me of a recent case in which he had driven no less than seven devils from the body of a patient, each time with the same effect.

He showed me long lists of patients who had been successfully treated. He said that over a great number of years some sixty thousand patients had come to him. Then he showed me literally thousands upon thousands of charms which patients had been wearing without effect, and which they had left with him, when he had cured them by casting out their devils. The charms were tied up in bundles of forty or fifty and were left hanging from nails around the sides of the building. In corners there were piles of sticks and crutches which had been left by those whose lameness had been cured.

The whole scene seemed just too fantastic – a little black boy
working the hand pump at the old drum of water, and the bishop in
black robes and golden crucifix hosing out devils and banging the
patients on the head with his wooden cross. Yet I know of no
psychiatrist who could produce such tangible evidence of success. A
partial explanation lies in the fact that the form in which nervous
illness manifests itself is to some extent dependent on cultural
influences. A good example of this is the way in which nervous
illness in the First World War showed itself in cardiac symptoms in a
condition which became known as D.A.H. – Disordered Action of
the Heart. In the Second World War this condition was practically
unknown, and nervous illness was manifested predominantly in
dyspeptic symptoms and open anxiety. Primitive peoples tend to
manifest nervous illness in hysterical symptoms such as paralysis of
limbs. This type of hysteria is often relieved quite easily by any
dramatic method of treatment. In our culture the authoritative use of
hypnosis or the intravenous injection of a barbiturate drug is often
used. The main problem is that, if the symptom is just removed in
this way without anything being done to relieve the underlying
anxiety which causes the symptom, there is a likelihood of other
symptoms arising. I do not know anything of the relapse rate among
the bishop's patients, but by any standards he must surely be
regarded as one of the great healers of modern times, even if he does
work among people whose nervous illness is relatively easily
relieved by dramatic methods.

By the time he had finished explaining all this to me, people were
beginning to file into the shed and seat themselves on the pews.
They were coming for his Sunday afternoon service. It was a motley
crowd, if ever there was one. Most of the people were poor, because
nearly everyone in Ethiopia is poor. But when people are both poor
and sick there is real destitution. Yet in the crowd there was a
sprinkling of well-dressed men and women. Some were obviously
very ill, and came in supported by others on each side of them. Some
were carried in, and two or three were brought along on stretchers.
The bishop, with me at his side, stood by the pulpit. Many came up
to him and he offered them his crucifix to kiss. A chair was brought
for me and placed in front of the pulpit. The bishop mounted the
steps to the pulpit and commenced the service. There were some
hymns and a long sermon in which he maintained the attention of
all who were present. As I was unable to understand a word of what
he was saying, I sat there absorbed by the facial expressions of those
before me. There, in those ramshackle surroundings, listening to a
man whose theological concepts seemed tawdry in the extreme, I
saw hope and calm in the faces of those who were otherwise
destitute. He was confident. He knew no doubts. Nor did he know
humility. In fact, he had a childish conceit about him. But in spite of
his conceit there was obvious sincerity. He had helped a hundred
times as many patients as I shall ever help in my professional life.
And for this I respect him.

Whatever one may think of that bishop and his methods of exorcism, he has a lot in common in many ways with some present-day exorcists, and it must seem likely that the combination of showmanship, domination, religious fervour, conceit and sincerity has a lot to do with successful exorcism.

Belief in demonic possession was widespread in early Christian times, when possessing 'devils' were thought to be 'spirits of the wicked dead', but no less bizarre cases come to light at the present time. In 1981 an American correspondent and friend sent me details of a very strange case that came to court in Brookfield, Connecticut, and was reported in the *Los Angeles Times*, dated 8 March 1981. I cannot do better than quote extracts from the relevant issue (and I cannot but admire the opening sentence!):

> The devil appears headed for his day in court in this tranquil Connecticut town and the charge is murder. The bizarre story encompasses attempts by Catholic priests to rid an 11-year-old boy of 'demons', a 19-year-old friend who challenged those 'demons' to 'take me on' and now being held in a stabbing death, and a criminal lawyer who says he will use 'demonic possession' as a defence.
>
> It all started last summer when psychic researchers and priests worked diligently in a secluded Cape Cod-style home to rid the boy of 'demons' they said had taken over his body. The friend, Arne Cheyenne Johnson, who lived at the house and witnessed the sessions, challenged the demons: 'Control me, leave the boy alone', according to tape recordings of the sessions. Now, Johnson is being held under $125,000 bond in Bridgeport in the stabbing of Alan Bono. A grand jury will hear the case and if Johnson is indicted, his attorney says he is prepared to argue that 'the devil made Mr Johnson do it'. 'The courts have dealt with existence of God; now they're going to have to deal with the existence of the devil,' stated the lawyer, Martin Minnella.
>
> Johnson, a slender, muscular youth with curly blond hair and a spotless criminal record, worked for a tree surgeon. He and Bono were 'the best of friends', according to those who knew them both. Police say Bono received multiple stab wounds during a quarrel with Johnson in front of the dog kennels Bono managed. Johnson's folding knife, with a five-inch blade, was recovered from the scene. He was arrested a few miles away.
>
> Minnella said he was prepared to produce tapes, photographs and expert testimony – from priests and psychic researchers – to show that Johnson was overtaken by the devil and not responsible for his acts. 'We have substantial, credible evidence that Mr Johnson had no intent to harm anyone and what happened was a result of demonic

possession,' Minnella said. 'People may not really want to deal with
the devil, but he exists.'

Lorraine and Ed Warren, the psychic researchers concerned in the
case, backed up the lawyer. 'We've always felt that if they ever bring
us into a court of law, we will prove that the preternatural exists –
that the devil exists,' they said. It was the Warrens who were
associated with the so-called Amityville Horror, in which a Long
Island family fled from their Long Island home, claiming to have
been harassed by supernatural forces.

The family in the present case asked the Warrens in 1980 to help
their 11-year-old son, who appeared to be 'possessed'. The Warrens
brought a local priest and a doctor with them to investigate the
matter. They said they found 'movement of objects and other
frightening manifestations' in the house. Tape recordings were
made of some of the sessions and the boy is heard making guttural
and hissing sounds, cursing his mother, and threatening to stab and
kill those present in the room.

During the summer of 1980 Johnson 'prayed with the boy and
slept in the same room', Mrs Warren said; and three times they had
encountered what the family had come to call 'the beast'.

The Warrens and Johnson's lawyer maintained that a fourth
encounter came on 16 February 1981 and that was when Johnson
became involved in the fatal quarrel. 'He went all out to help this
little lad', Warren said at the time. 'Day after day. And what is his
reward? He's sitting in jail charged with murdering a man he liked, a
man he never intended to kill ...'

But perhaps we are transgressing from the subject of
exorcism.

The remarkably successful 1973 film *The Exorcist*, based on a
best-selling book by William Peter Blatty, resulted in a definite
increase in the number of people who considered themselves to
be possessed. In 1980 *The Exorcist* was placed fourth in a list of
the highest grossing films ever produced – by the American
trade paper *Variety*. Blatty's novel was the story of a girl
possessed and eventually exorcized by a Jesuit priest. *The
Exorcist* had a basis in fact, but the final production was
distorted out of all recognition.

The genuine case on which *The Exorcist* was based began in
the middle of January 1949, in a suburb of Washington, when a
14-year-old-old boy complained of hearing unexplained
scratching sounds around his bed at night. The same thing
happened the next night, and the night after that. Two weeks
later, during which time there had been no abatement of the
disturbances, the boy's aunt in St Louis died. The boy and also

his grandmother began to wonder whether the noises might have some connection with her death and, when the scratching noises came again, they asked: 'Is that you, Aunt Tillie? If it is, knock three times.' Immediately they heard three loud knocks.

Soon the boy was actually being scratched while he was in bed, and some of the marks appeared to represent words. Most people are reluctant to accept such marks ('stigmata') as being due to any external influence, and it has been scientifically established that stigmata can be induced and created by the mind. Swellings have appeared on the bodies of mentally ill people who believe they have complaints that cause swellings; under hypnosis blisters have appeared when a person has been told that a lighted cigarette is touching them when in fact it is the end of a pencil; similar effects have been obtained when a person is touched by a book and told it is a red-hot iron. However, in the Washington household there were other mysterious happenings. Bedclothes would suddenly rear up and then collapse, and at other times clothing would stand stiffly erect as though it were starched; when anyone approached, it collapsed. Objects would be hurled around the bedroom.

The family were Lutherans, and on 17 February 1949 the somewhat sceptical pastor of the local church took the boy into his own house. There he saw for himself the boy's bed vibrate and the mattress undulate; he also saw a chair, with the boy seated on it, move across a room and rise up. Puzzled and completely baffled by the happenings, he decided that a psychiatrist might be able to suggest a solution or a course of action, and the boy was taken to Georgetown University Medical Centre. The psychiatrists admitted that they were equally baffled and, somewhat surprisingly, the pastor went back to the family and advised them to consult a Roman Catholic priest.

The boy returned home, and the house was blessed on 9 March 1949 by the Catholic priest, who fixed a relic of St Mary Margaret at the head of the boy's bed. While the priest was still in the house, carrying out his ceremonies, the bed began to move by itself. The following night more disturbances occurred and the relic was torn from the bed and thrown at a mirror.

On 11 March 1949 the boy and the house received a 'blessing' which involved a relic of St Francis Xavier, and then the boy was moved to a Jesuit residence at St Louis. Father William Bowden, pastor of the Collegiate Church of St Louis, together with two other priests, was then authorized to perform a service of exorcism. By all accounts it was a long and arduous rite, lasting practically the whole night, during which the boy repeatedly shouted obscenities, when he was not chattering in strange languages, and then he became violent and abusive. However, before morning he had been declared to be cured, and that really was the end of the matter. That boy is today a successful businessman and married with three children.

Such was the case, as reported by the Catholic Truth Society, which Blatty used as a basis for his book, which was, in fact, far too sensational, and those who have studied exorcism found it totally unbelievable. His fictional exorcist initiated his own destruction by challenging the 'demon' possessing the child to 'try something bigger': inviting it to leave the child and invade him instead: an identical invitation occurred in *Amityville 2*, a 1982 film so packed with contrived horrors that to any informed person it bordered on farce. Such a challenge would never have been made by an authorized Roman Catholic exorcist, who, according to the rules governing such rites approved by the Vatican, 'must be properly distinguished for his piety, prudence and integrity of life'.

Blatty was, of course, entitled to use fiction to create the utmost impact, but the resulting film worried many priests and exorcists throughout the world. 'Demons' were suddenly in fashion, and susceptible people were quick to imagine them or to see symptoms which, to their satisfaction, established them. Parents were worried that unusual behaviour in their children, which previously might have been regarded as a character defect, could be a sign of 'possession', and soon after *The Exorcist* film was released (1973) there were a number of tragedies in America that might well be associated with the film, described by film writer and critic Kim Newman as 'a simplistic, overinflated shocker that reduces potentially interesting themes to banality'.

The film, with its crucifix masturbation, 180-degree head-turning, gruff-voiced swearing and extensive vomiting, portrayed an unequivocally evil demon corrupting an innocent little girl. In the finale, the priests' faith triumphs as they sacrifice their lives to free the victim.

As Victoria Branden has pointed out (*Understanding Ghosts*), after the film exorcists popped up all over the place; epileptic fits, for example, were thought to be an indication of the work of the Devil, and the only certain cure was through exorcism. Such a trend can be very dangerous: if you believe that an illness is caused by demons instead of by other causes, you go to an exorcist instead of to a doctor, and you are in trouble.

In fairness, some Roman Catholic priests were pleased with the film. The Rev. John J. Nicola praised *The Exorcist* because, he said, 'I feel kind of satisfied that the triumph of faith has come across ...' Victoria Branden comments: 'Faith, in this context, is apparently demonstrated by belief in the devil's power to cause mental illness. A further oddity of the human mind is some people's insistence that to deny such diabolical meddling is to betray an irreligious nature. It is a kind of reverse-side of belief in miracles of healing, which still occur, as sensationally as they did in Biblical times, often through traditional religious patterns such as pilgrimages to holy places, often through lay healers like Canadians Katherine Kuhlman and Oral Roberts. The sceptics ask why God should afflict the sufferer in the first place, if only to heal him later in a rather melodramatic way. Sufferers and healers ignore such questions, or answer that only in terms of the necessity for faith and the mystery of God.'

There is no accounting for people's believing in such enigmatic happenings: illness inflicted by evil spirits, cures effected by divine intervention, often in answer to prayer; one either accepts such happenings or denies that they do happen.

Whatever one feels about the film *The Exorcist* and the way in which it dealt with a serious subject, from a film-buff's point of view it was the first horror film since the 1930s (with the possible exception of *Rosemary's Baby*) to be a serious contender for Academy Awards. In the end it lost out on its acting, direction, visual and best film nominations and obtained Oscars 'only' for best sound and best screenplay (by the author of the novel), but the film did bring horror films back to the attention of the major studios, and it spawned a host of low-budget imitations, mostly made in Italy, and concentrating on the profanity and sickening aspects of the film.

Incidentally, or perhaps ironically, the actress who played the devil-possessed child in *The Exorcist* had a tragic aftermath: after her moment of nubile fame she plunged into a sordid nightmare of promiscuous sex and drugs. 'Her own teenage years turned into something of a horror movie,' says Marianne Sinclair in her volume *Hollywood Lolita*.[3]

At one stage there she was, still a little teenage nymphet, having to hide both from the F.B.I., hot on her trail in connection with a drug peddling ring, and from some mad gunman who claimed to have already killed one actor, and who believed that Linda Blair was a devil-possessed nymphomaniac.' Eventually the actress was sentenced to three years probation for conspiring to possess cocaine.

I was told a strange tale of possession and exorcism by Leslie Watkins, when he attended a Ghost Club meeting as a guest of a member a few years ago, a tale corroborated and enlarged upon on another occasion by Captain Eric Myers, the Ghost Club member in question. In his book *The Real Exorcists*, Watkins relates the story and calls the young married man concerned 'Keith', and he states that for no less than six years, by the time he met Keith, psychiatrists had been trying unsuccessfully to help him and to relieve emotional difficulties which he felt were caused by a demon obsessed by violence.

Keith said he had had visions ever since he was a small child: '… not dreams but people and things that come to me when I'm wide awake, sometimes in the middle of the day, and stay for a while before suddenly disappearing. Some of them are monstrous things, huge and black and obscene, which taunt me and try to goad me into awful violence.'

The psychiatrists regarded Keith as a potentially aggressive neurotic and gave him tranquillizers; eventually they admitted there was nothing more they could do for him, and when he heard that, Keith asked about exorcism. He was told it could do no harm, and in August 1981 four 'casting-out' ceremonies were performed by Father John Wheaton with additional help.

Afterwards Keith said he had seen visions of himself as he was in an earlier life, in England hundreds of years ago, and he seemed to be a kind of 'witch-hunter'; he was certainly very powerful and often cruel. He apparently enjoyed persecuting people and having them tortured. In the end he was betrayed and killed in a most agonizing way. And the evil that was in him then he felt was still inside him …

He began to be in the habit of indicating the lower part of his chest: 'I can feel it here, distinctly, as something separate from me; it's difficult to describe but this is something evil without a doubt.' This 'something of evil', Keith claimed, often tried to force him into acts of violence or destruction. It urged him to lash out at people and to destroy things. It also tried to persuade him to injure himself. Repeatedly he found himself about to stab a knife into one of his eyes. Usually he managed to resist the strong urge in time, but sometimes things became so difficult that he was in a constant state of turmoil, and he became desperate to get rid of whatever was 'possessing' him.

Once 'it' tried to attack Keith's wife, and he had an awful job stopping himself. He finished up not hitting her but punching his fist through the glass panel of a door. Frightened of 'its' suddenly making its presence felt, he could never be at ease with other people, frightened that 'it' was going to make him do something dreadful.

Satisfied that a full exorcism was called for and having made all the necessary arrangements, Keith, Leslie Watkins and Father Wheaton went into the chapel of Our Lady in Exeter. It should perhaps be explained that Father Wheaton is a priest in the Liberal Catholic Church, an autonomous church which is independent of Rome, its Holy Orders being derived from the Old Catholic Church of Holland, and it is a constituent part of the One Holy Catholic and Apostolic Church.

Keith took his place facing a Madonna, and early in the ceremony he was required to stand with bowed head while Father Wheaton sprinkled him with holy water and anointed him with oil and incense. This done, the priest intoned: 'May the Cross of the Son of God, who is mightier than all the hosts of Satan and more glorious than all the angels of Heaven, abide with you in your going out and your coming in; by day and by night, at morning and at evening, at all times and in all places, may it protect and defend you; from the wrath of evil man, from the assaults of evil spirits, from foes visible and invisible, from the snares of the Devil, from all low passions that beguile the soul and body, may it guard, protect and deliver you ...'

At this point in the casting-out ceremony Keith gave a gasp and appeared to be in some distress. He seemed to have difficulty in keeping an upright position and, for the first time at any exorcism, Leslie Watkins told me, he was conscious of what he described as 'an extraordinary vibrancy'. It was almost as though the atmosphere in the chapel had become charged with electricity. Meanwhile Keith began shaking his head from side to side and mumbling something that sounded like, 'You haven't got rid of it, you haven't got rid of it ...' After a moment he lifted his head and spoke to Father Wheaton: 'You've weakened it and it began to leave me but you haven't got rid of it and now it's back again ...'

The three men took a rest and then returned to the chapel, and the ritual was repeated. This time there was nothing like the atmosphere and the tension of the previous occasion. The priest made his healing gestures and intoned the words of exorcism while Keith stood with bowed head and closed eyes.

'That made no impact at all,' Keith said afterwards. 'It was nothing like the first time when I could feel something inside me struggling ... yes, it quite definitely seems weaker than it was. I don't feel up to going through all that again today but I would like you to try again ...'

On his way home Keith said afterwards he had to exert all his self-control to prevent 'it' from causing him to jump out of the window of the moving train. Just over a week later Father Wheaton tried again. This time Keith took precautions. He was determined not to risk being forced to throw himself from a moving train, and two friends drove him to Exeter.

This third service of exorcism, which began with such high hopes, was completely uneventful, and afterwards Keith shook his head. 'I don't know ...' he said. 'I think you reached "it" but I really don't know.'

'In that case,' said Father Wheaton, after they had all had a rest, 'we'll do it again ...'

They returned to the chapel. Nothing unusual seemed to happen during that fourth ceremonial service until, nearly at the end, there was an extraordinary transformation in Keith. He sat down suddenly, then rocked backwards and forwards, with his hands covering his face, and then suddenly he strode across the chapel and slouched against the far wall. He looked up, glancing contemptuously at the altar, and then his menacing look turned towards Father Wheaton: 'I'm going to pull this place down brick by brick!' he snarled, his eyes full of loathing. As he spoke, his face became distorted with hatred, and his voice, usually soft and gentle, was rasping and hard and coarse-sounding. 'This pathetic little chapel of yours ... I'm going to destroy it utterly ...'

Five candles were burning on the altar. Keith took a couple of steps towards them, as if to start his promised destruction, but then he paused to sneer at Father Wheaton: 'You're lost, priest! You with your idiot prattling ... you've been wasting your time ...' Father Wheaton swallowed hard and then, collecting his thoughts, moved towards Keith and spoke with quiet authority: 'You'd better sit down ...' Before he could say any more, 'Get back!' screamed Keith, clenching his fists and adopting an aggressive attitude. 'Keep away, priest, or I'll cripple you for life ...'

Father Wheaton was once a London policeman, and he knew how to deal with threats of violence. He maintained an air of unruffled calm. He stretched out his arms, as if to embrace Keith, and he moved closer. Keith suddenly lowered his head, and all the bluster and aggression went out of him. His body sagged, and despair and remorse marked his face. 'I'm sorry ... I really am sorry ...' Tears welled up in his eyes, and his distress was blatantly genuine. 'I know what I said, but, please believe me, it wasn't me saying it ...' He sat down meekly and Father Wheaton gently cradled his head and prayed quietly. Keith continued to apologize and plead for forgiveness as everyone retired to a nearby room. There Keith was sad and disillusioned. 'I think we should face it,' he said at last. 'We're not getting anywhere. There's no point in trying any more.'

Even Father Wheaton had to admit that he was baffled and did not know what to do next. In the end it was agreed to seek the advice of Father Arnold Clare, an experienced exorcist and clairvoyant.

On 23 August 1981 Keith visited the Devon home of Father Clare, who, during the previous two days, had been praying for guidance and making preparations for Keith's visit. He questioned Keith briefly, and then the party adjourned to a small private chapel where, using holy water and incense, Father Clare performed a short ceremony of exorcism, not dissimilar to those performed by Father Wheaton. Afterwards he explained that this service was an 'antiseptic precaution', for he was already convinced that Keith's problems were caused by a 'psychic or emotional bottleneck'.

Keith visited Father Clare several more times, but within two months he appeared to be free of his inner turmoil. The outcome was satisfactory, although the various ceremonies of exorcism had seemingly failed – or had they served a useful purpose? It is worth noting that Keith was not harmed in any way by the exorcisms. He had sought the help of the Church because of the hope it seemed to offer; this in turn led him to the 'spiritual healing' which, it appears, was more successful than the prolonged efforts of psychiatrists.

Possession is not always obvious and, as in the case of 'Keith', it may not be possession that is affecting the so-called possessed person. We soon find ourselves in difficult waters. C.S. Lewis once pointed out to me, when I mentioned that, if the Devil existed, he must be very clever, that the Devil's most effective strategy is to pretend that he does not exist – this is even more effective than disguising himself as an angel of light!

It has to be recognized that hallucination plays a part in inducing the state of possession, and the critical T.K. Oesterreich, after much study of the phenomenon of possession in many parts of the world, came to the conclusion that on occasion the subject's organism does seem to be invaded by a new personality which subsists there in place of or side by side with the normal personality of the subject – and the successful exorcism of demons, or whatever may be possessing a subject, is due to the power of belief.

On that sobering note we will leave the problem of possession and exorcism, for the moment.

5   Exorcism and Witchcraft

The late Ronald Seth once told me that his researches into witchcraft had resulted in his acceptance of an ancient cure for bewitchment – by white magic: 'If a child is bewitched, take a candle and throw it three times through an enchanted hoop, ring or belt, and then a dog must throw it and then shake the belt over a fire; then throw it down on the ground and leave it there until a dog or a cat walks over it; and sickness of all kinds will leave the person and enter the dog or cat ...' I dare say it is as good an exorcism as many another.

On actual exorcism in respect of witchcraft, he was in favour of simple Christian exorcism: 'Fix your eyes firmly on the afflicted person and, laying a hand on his or her head, call upon the devil who is the originator of evil; make the sign of the cross over the affected person and urge the devil to depart, saying: "In the name of Jesus Christ I command you, unclean spirit, if you hide in the body of this man [or woman or child] created by God, if you vex him [or her] in any way, at once give me some sign of the certainty of your presence in this child of God, which until now in my absence you have been able to do as you and your master wish." If some sign is accepted as evidence of the presence of an evil spirit, the exorcist calls upon the almighty power of Jesus Christ and commands whoever is vexing the bewitched person to, "Go hence, nor pester or annoy or trouble this person or anyone here present from this moment forward – Go now!" '

Such exorcisms or something like them have a long history. St Paul is said to have exorcized evil spirits in the name of the Father, Son and Holy Ghost. In the New Testament a comparable formula is to be found in St Matthew, but here it is generally regarded as a doctrinal expansion of some simpler form, such as 'in my name', the speaker being Jesus himself; for there is no hint of such a formula elsewhere in the New Testament.

In the Middle Ages devils and demons and Satan himself were very real and ever-present beings. Much of the literature of the period shows traces of monks' and nuns' and other pious persons' preoccupation with the doings of Satan and his angels. It can be argued that primitive peoples were less concerned or aware of such matters, although it cannot but be accepted that the monastic conceptions of the Devil, his followers and his works had definite roots in earlier beliefs.

Dr G.G. Coulton, who was regarded as possessing an unsurpassed knowledge of the Middle and Dark Ages, has shown in his book, *Five Centuries of Religion*, that this intense and overwhelming belief in the power of demons was due to the fact that during the previous cultures a theory had been accepted which asserted that by the fall of man the world had become the Devil's property.

A sense of the considerable 'reality' gained by the Devil is evident in a number of works published during the twelfth and thirteenth centuries, notably the *Processus Belial* and the *Processus Sathanae*.

The former, usually ascribed to twelfth-century Hugh St Victor, takes the form of a dialogue between God and the Devil in which they dispute for the soul of man in a series of legalistic arguments. For example, God, intending to redeem the world through a man, came into the world and found the Devil ruling over the whole world, but it was God's world, for He had made it; yet it could be argued that it was the Devil's, for he now possessed it. God in the beginning had created the world, and from the beginning the Devil had possessed it; therefore a struggle began between God and the Devil.

The argument continued: God claimed to be taking what was His; the Devil refused to be deprived of what he held in his power after it had been so long neglected by God. God replied that the Devil had fraudently taken and was violently holding that which was not his own; to which the Devil retorted that God had neither gainsaid him when he took it nor ever sought it back while he held it. God claimed the power of using force, if He would, to regain His own; the Devil answered that force should not be abused against justice. All this is but the beginning of a long series of arguments intended to show the

Devil's empire over men and why he cannot be dispossessed by God without a thoroughly legal form of atonement.

The possession of man by the Devil is affirmed by Peter Lombard (1100–1160) in his *Four Books of Sentences*, a work devoted to the creation and the fall of the angels. He does have a somewhat crude idea of the work of Jesus, for he says, 'Mankind had fallen into the hands of the prince of the world, who seduced Adam and enslaved him, and began to possess us as born bondmen; but the Redeemer came and the Deceiver was conquered. What then did the Redeemer do to our Captivator? He set him His own cross as a mousetrap, and laid his own blood there as a bait.'

Such expressions of the Devil's claim upon man were common, and it is not surprising that all classes of people generally, and the monks in particular, were obsessed by the thought of the hostile operations of demons. In the thirteenth century evidence for the visible and tangible presence of God was looked for far oftener than in our own time, although the omnipresence of the Devil was realized at the same time, perhaps with disproportionate vividness. 'Flashes of blinding spiritual light alternated with a horror of great darkness,' says Dr Coulton. 'Much of what is most harsh and repulsive in early Protestantism is a direct legacy of this medieval Satanology.'

Devils were everywhere, plain to the eye in ordinary and innocent operations of nature: they rode on the thunderstorm and filled the winter twilight with cawing, as the rooks made their way home to roost; a sparrow, chancing to fly in through a window, was the fiend incarnate. Thousands of invisible devils were thought to besiege one tiny Franciscan hermitage, and the friars would be seen, day after day, brandishing their sticks in the air and driving them away like flies. But it was the visible Devil that was most feared, for there was always the possibility that he might be lurking under the disguise of an angel of light, of the Virgin Mary, of 'Our Lord Himself' ... Monks and friars, it should be explained, were given the power of second sight, enabling them to perceive the presence of demons.

One thirteenth-century book (by a disciple of the Abbot Richalm)[1] might almost be regarded as a complete handbook of medieval demonology. 'It is marvellous that any one of us should still be alive,' Richalm is quoted as saying, 'and were it not for God's grace, not one of us would escape. Demons ride like particles of dust in the sunbeam; they are scattered everywhere like dust; they come down upon us like rain; their multitude fills the whole world, the whole air; yes, the whole air is a thick mass of devils.'

Devils, it was said, caused drunkenness when no wine had been consumed; they caused coughing and flatulence; they crept into the teeth and made them ache; they swarmed under garments 'with the bodily semblance and the bloodthirsty appetite of fleas', so the victim was tempted 'to scratch himself after an unseemly fashion' and the Devil had gained a petty triumph. In particular, attack by demons at the moment of death was greatly feared, for the demons were anxious to wrest the immortal soul from the dying man.

Petrus Diacanus, in his *Chronicle of Monte Casion*, tells of a French nobleman who had lived a sinful life but repented and took refuge in a monastery. 'When he came to die, he called together the brethren of the monastery and besought that he be clothed in monastic habit as protection. Soon after he had put on these holy vestments, he gave up the ghost; and no sooner had the man's soul left his body than a terrible horde of demons bound it with burning chains and sought to drag it down into the flames of hell when the blessed Father of the monastery appeared with his pastoral staff in his hand and he vanquished the demons.'

There are many such stories to show that such diabolical delusions were most to be feared at the moment of death, for it was known that the Devil '... doth attack men most vehemently at their latter end, knowing that if he conquer them, his victory is final'. Even the saints were sometimes said to see devils at their death, '... as we see in the case of Christ ... and in that which we read of the Mother of God, though in an apocryphal history, how all her life long she besought her son that He would deign, at the moment of death, to guard her from that vision of demons'.

From such beliefs it is a small step to accepting the possibility of demons inhabiting the bodies of some persons and of its being possible to exorcize such demons. The history of witchcraft is full of accounts of men being attacked by demons in the forms of various creatures. Thus, according to St Gregory the Enlightener (*c.* 240–*c.* 326), '... three great flies, of exceeding blackness, were seen to leave one man's mouth at the moment of his delivery; from another the Devil slunk out in the form of a dog. One frustrated demon sought to avenge himself on the exorcizing monk by entering the dormitory that night in the form of a crow, and was about to slip into the sleeping victim's mouth, when the latter awoke, called instinctively upon his patron, and had not even finished the first syllable of "Benedict" before the demon was already out of the window again!'

The thirteenth-century volume already referred to[2] contains chapters headed: 'Concerning the Multitude of Demons; How Demons trip up Men; How Demons Speak; Demons Deform Bodies; Demons Assume Forms Congruous to their Works' and, perhaps most frightening of all, 'Those to Whom the Devil Came in the Forms of Saints Francis, Anthony, Clare, Agnes, the Virgin Mary and of Christ himself'.

The gods of the pagan peoples were accepted by the Fathers of the early Church as real beings – not gods but evil spirits; one frequent citation from the Bible being the saying of the Psalmist: 'For all the gods of the peoples are demons.' Were these gods of the pagan world, reduced by Christian belief to the rank of demons, incorporated into the vast system of magic and witchcraft? The Christian missionaries evangelized the unbelieving peoples but inevitably the pagan minds were imbued with the old beliefs, and as the new converts became preachers, they retained many of their old ideas, and many pagan beliefs became absorbed into Christianity.

Not that so-called black magic and witchcraft sprang up as a new creation in the Middle Ages. We know that these practices were banned from time to time by the pagan emperors of Rome; Nero and Caracalle, for instance, both severely persecuted those who practised such activities and held such beliefs. During the course of his monumental *Inquisition of the Middle Ages* (1888), H.C. Lea says: 'To perform or to procure the performance of impious nocturnal rites with the object of bewitching anyone was punished with the severest penalties known to the Roman law – crucifixion or the beasts ... Accomplices in magical practices were subjected to crucifixion or the beasts, while magicians themselves were burned alive. The knowledge of the art was forbidden as well as its exercise: all books of magic were to be burned, and their owners subjected to deportation or capital punishment, according to their rank.'

When the Church came to be regarded as supreme and to control to a great extent the machinery of government, it soon turned its attention to the empire of Satan. Soon the practice of witchcraft became punishable with death. St Theodore (Archbishop of Canterbury 668–90) penalized those who practised witchcraft, although, for a time at any rate, the Church appears to have lacked either the will or the power effectively to suppress those forbidden rites. The fact was of course, that the Church itself was imbued with pagan practises, and in the eighth century, to quote one example, St Boniface had to suppress Bishop Adalbert who taught the invocation of the angels Uriel, Raguel, Tubuel, Inias, Tubuas, Sabaoe and Simiel. Adalbert, incidentally, was later venerated as a saint, and the chippings of his nails and hair were to become treasured relics. Then in 745 in Rome Pope Zachary declared this false worship of angels to be a worship of demons; even so, it lingered on for another three centuries.

The first papal bull (an official and authoritative document issued by Rome) to be aimed directly at witchcraft and the black arts seems to be that of Alexander IV on 13 December 1258, addressed to the Franciscan inquisitors. Witchcraft is further mentioned in a papal bull of 1317, during the course of which Pope John XXII complains that men of his Court, and even his own physician, '... had given themselves over to the Devil, and had conjured evil spirits into rings, looking-glasses, and circles, in order to influence men both at a distance and also near at hand ... Yes, that his enemies even had availed themselves of means of sorcery in order to dispatch him out of the world.' Ten years later the same Pope was to complain that there prevailed '... such a darkness that many have forsaken the true light and have made a compact with hell, and demand of the demons speech and answer ...'. By the end of the fourteenth century great efforts were being made by the Church to overcome what was felt to be the 'great evil' of witchcraft.

However, there are grounds for regarding the beginning of the modern persecution of witchcraft as dating from the papal bull of Innocent VIII, published on 5 December 1484. In giving formal sanction to the prosecution of witches, it placed a deadly instrument in the hands of the now practically all-powerful Church.

It has come to our ears [says the pontiff], not without immense trouble and grief to ourselves, that in some parts of Higher Germany ... very many persons of both sexes, deviating from the Catholic faith, abuse themselves with the demons, Incubus and Succubus; and by incantations, charms, conjurations, and other wicked superstitions, by criminal acts and offences have caused the offspring of women and of the lower animals, the fruits of the earth, the grape, and the products of various plants, men, women and other animals of different kinds, vineyards, meadows, pasture land, corn and other vegetables of the earth, to perish, be oppressed and utterly destroyed; that they tortured men and women with cruel pains and torments, internal as well as external; that they hinder the proper intercourse of the sexes, and the propagation of the human species. Moreover, they are in the habit of denying the very faith itself. We, therefore, willing to provide by opportune remedies according as it falls to us by our office, by our apostolical authority, by the tenor of these presents do appoint and decree that they be convicted, imprisoned, punished, and mulcted according to their offences ...

Five years later the famous 'Hammer of Witches', the *Malleus Maleficarum* (1489), laid out rules for the detection and prosecution of witches, detailing 1. Things that pertain to witchcraft; 2. The effects of witchcraft; and 3. The remedies for witchcraft. No less an authority than the Rev. Montague Summers stated, 'Certain it is that the *Malleus Maleficarum* is the most solid, the most important work in the whole vast library of witchcraft.'

The persecution and slaughter of witches began immediately and continued without interruption until the end of the seventeenth century. If the number of witches is any indication of the extent of the practice, witchcraft must have been rampant everywhere. Unfortunately the truth is, of course, that many thousands of completely innocent people, old and young, male and female, perished at the hands of the Church. No one can read contemporary accounts of witchcraft without realizing that countless people were condemned and lost their lives on the flimsiest of pretences. J.H. Crehan SJ, who wrote a memoir of Herbert Thurston SJ and edited Thurston's famous study *Ghosts and Poltergeists*, told me at a meeting of the Society for Psychical Research that Herbert Thurston thought that in ninety-nine cases out of a hundred the allegations rested upon nothing but pure delusion. And, of course, the cruellest tortures were applied in ways that defeat all the ends of justice.

Be that as it may, up to the middle of the seventeenth century there are detailed examples of witchcraft and the alleged exorcisms of demons controlling witches. In a volume published in Paris in 1575 there is an illustration depicting a demon leaving the body of a woman while a bishop is administering the Eucharist. The woman's mouth is forced open to receive the consecrated wafer, and the 'unclean spirit' is shown leaving her in the form of a little demon with claws – and it is these little demons that are the most pernicious, we are told!

Cardinal Richelieu himself sent the Rev. Pére Surin to the convent of the Ursulines at Loudun to exorcise the demons there – an evil which had lasted several years. His predecessors in this task had managed only to dislodge three demons from the bodies of three nuns, although the demon Asmodeus had been one of them and he had been expelled after writing and signing a deed attesting the event; a manuscript that is still preserved in the Bibliothéque Nationale.

Pére Surin set about expelling the 'numerous demons' that possessed the mother Prioress, which he apparently did, one by one, all faithfully recorded in folios still preserved, one badly damaged and seeming to bear traces of scorching – hell-fire perhaps? The demons so expelled revealed that they were seraphin and cherubim and fallen thrones (the third of the nine orders of angels in the celestial hierarchy).

The Jesuit exorcist had to undergo violent assault against his person, and several times he was inhabited by demons himself. 'Once,' he says 'the demons devised a horrible charm by the power of which the Mother Prioress became quite other than she really was for the space of eight days; her countenance became of a rare beauty. On another day the demon, assuming my shape, entered the parlour and in a gentle voice, like mine, talked to the Mother with the intent of leading her astray ... and in plain fact there was every appearance of it,' says Pére Surin. 'But upon the day of the Circumcision in the year 1635 the demon said that the Holy Virgin had forced him so to do as that the Mother should cast up all the humours which were causing the seeming pregnancy. So it was that she vomited them during the exorcism within the space of two hours, where of several persons of quality were witness, and among others the Bishop of Nîmes.'

The Surin exorcisms became an interminable series of

adventures, sometimes tragic but more often grotesque. The 'demons' whipped the nuns and terrified them with horrible threats and assaults; at other times the nuns appeared to have had bestowed upon them the gift of tongues, when 'the most unlettered' would discourse at length in Latin; at other times again the nuns would be set off into peals of laughter during offices and prayers and, 'more serious still', found themselves stirred to 'quite unseemly thoughts'.

Some of the demons left marks as they fled. Leviathan left a red cross upon the forehead of the mother prioress, in accordance with a contract the demon had made with the bishop of Poitiers. The demon Isacaron left on the hand of the mother prioress, 'in full sight of everyone', the sacred name 'Maria' in Roman letters, deeply graven into the flesh, 'accompanied by the name "St Joseph" in smaller characters'.

The tortures were condoned by the results, and St Remigius (*c.* 438–533), who condemned and executed 900 witches, gives as an argument why tortures should be used: '... that scarce anyone was known to be brought to repentance and confession but by these means and therefore,' he says, 'their pains are their blessings.'

It is this complete blindness on the part of the inquisitors and judges that makes it so difficult to decide what measure of truth there may be in the so-called 'confessions' of those accused of witchcraft. In numbers alone the victims of witchcraft are frightening: 500 perished in Geneva in three months in 1515, and the same blood-letting took place in Germany, Spain, France, England and Scotland. And then it all passed. At one period, as various historians have pointed out, everyone seemed predisposed to believe in witches and witchcraft; at a later period we find that this predisposition has silently passed away, to leave behind it the recognition that belief in witchcraft could have been one of the most monstrous demonological conceptions; or was it a first resurgence of a religion far older than Christianity?

It has already been pointed out by more than one writer on the subject that witches were generally supposed to be avidly engaged in harming people and not merely putting demons inside them. Disease, coincidences and accidental death were all laid at the witches' door; barrenness, stillbirth, impotence were obvious choices but lesser misfortunes, such as soured milk or burned food, might also be blamed on witches. In fact, for centuries witchcraft was the scapegoat for any ills that befell mankind. It was blamed not only on a personal basis for illness, misfortune or disfigurement but also obliquely for harm done to a man's house or property, to his cattle and crops – whether by illness or adverse natural conditions; and it was also blamed for extremes in anything: the weather, plagues; defeat in battle; the list is endless. And then there was the use of witches as consultants and of witchcraft as a healer by black arts; belief in such activities being encouraged by the witches, with their claims to raise the dead; to metamorphose; to fly through the air; to transport themselves from one place to another; to control the elements; to levitate and so on.

One of the widespread beliefs during the heyday of witchcraft was that it was possible to infuse food with demons, an ability that was thought to be one of many magical powers conferred on witches by their satanic master. The witches' magic put a demon in the food, and the victim ate it – and thereby the demon entered the victim's body, from which it was extremely difficult to dislodge it. Thus a major aim of exorcism was to force the victim to vomit the original demon-bearing food.

As recently as 1920 Monsignor L. Cristiani, the French author of *Satan and the Modern World*, revealed that an exorcism was carried out in which the demon inhabiting a woman admitted that '... he had entered her, by means of a spell contrived by a wizard, in the form of a pellet of salt pork, washed down with a glass of white wine'. The affected woman was freed, we are told, when she vomited the pellet, 'a little ball of salt pork, about the size of a nut, with seven horns'.

Mention of vomiting in witches during exorcism reminds me of the story of the seventeenth-century 'Bilson Boy'. I have known Eric Maple, researcher, writer, lecturer and broadcaster on witchcraft, for many years (in 1963 he conducted his fellow Ghost Club members on a unique 'Journey into Witchcraft' through Essex), and during the course of a conversation after a club meeting he told me the story.

It has been described as 'perhaps the most fantastic case' in the history of witchcraft – or malingering – and it occurred in 1620, at the peak period of British witch-hunting; could it have been typical, one wonders? One day schoolboy William Perry returned to his home in Bilson (now Bilston), Staffordshire, exhibiting obvious signs of witchcraft: vomiting pins, feathers, wool, passing black (or blue) urine and generally acting as a bewitched person was 'known' to act. His parents' worst suspicions seemed to be confirmed when the boy admitted that he had been rude to an old woman, and when he had refused to apologize, she had pointed at him and mumbled words he could not understand. It seemed clear that he had been bewitched.

The Perrys were a Roman Catholic family, and understandably they sought aid from the local church who visited the house, saw the boy and, using holy water and repeated prayers, claimed to drive three evil spirits out of the boy's body, although, whenever Protestants were present, the devils, it was said, immediately re-entered the body of the boy, and the house was filled with screams and yells and oaths and violent denunciations of Martin Luther, Jean Calvin and John Fox, three prominent Protestant theologians of the previous century.

No time was lost in finding the 'old woman' who was thought to be responsible for bewitching the boy. This proved to be no difficulty, but she strenuously denied being a witch or having had anything to do with bewitching William Perry, although she admitted that she had muttered under breath after he had nearly knocked her over. She was put on trial but must have made a good impression, for in the middle of this period of witchcraft mania, she was found 'not guilty'.

The authorities now became suspicious of the boy, and he was removed to the home of Bishop Morton and there tested as to the genuineness of his apparent bewitchment. Pins were thrust into his fingers and toes, and he was struck on various parts of his body with a rod in an attempt to discover any insensitiveness to pain. All witches and those bewitched were thought to have at least one part of the body that was insensitive to pain, and the 'witch-finders' spent hours ingeniously exploring the most intimate parts of accused persons' bodies with needles and probes and pincers. Often a mole (especially if well hidden or of unusual shape) was more than sufficient to convince the examiners that they need seek no further. Equally an extra teat or anything that looked as though it might suckle a 'familiar', or some minor physical malformation, was to them proof positive. But the Bilson Boy seemed to pass the tests ...

And then, spied through the keyhole of his bedroom door, he was seen to pour blue ink into his chamber-pot! William knew the game was up, and he made a full confession and apologized publicly. He said the real villains were the Catholic priests, who had planned the whole scheme in order to bring to the attention of a wide public the merits of their Church. Taking advantage of the prevailing climate of opinion, they had persuaded the boy to pretend to be bewitched so that they could exhibit their skill at exorcism and deliver him from the 'devils that possessed him'.

Unfortunately for the Catholics, the Bilson Boy – in common with so many poltergeist children before and since – found that he enjoyed the attentions he received and the sensational attraction he became, and he refused to stop the act as he was supposed to after the Catholic exorcisms; and soon the whole matter was completely out of hand. A rare amusing incident in a period of vicious witch-hunting.

It has to be remembered that practically everyone in England at that time believed that human beings could harbour evil spirits, and the exorcism of such demons was an accepted function of the Churches. A case of the right man being in the right place at the right time was John Darrell, who became one of the best-known exorcists after a series of apparent successes.

John Darrell was an interesting man. Born in Mansfield in Nottinghamshire, he studied law at Cambridge before being ordained, and this lawyer-cum-priest came to prominence in 1586 when he exorcized a girl in his native town, a girl who had accused another woman of bewitching her. Darrell lent his not inconsiderable support to the girl in question but the charge was dismissed by the magistrate before whom the case was heard, and he went out of his way severely to reprimand Darrell for his part in the business, even threatening the priest with severe punishment if anything of a similar nature occurred again.

But John Darrell was not to be threatened. He ignored the warning and continued his exorcisms, specializing in driving demons out of children. He did, apparently, expel devils from several children, using his own brand of exorcism, fasting and prayers which, it was said, forced the demons to fly from bodies that were no longer able to offer nourishment to the parasitic little devils.

One case in which Darrell figured had far-reaching consequences. He and a companion exorcist claimed to drive a demon out of William Somers, a Nottingham boy, but for some reason the Church authorities became suspicious, investigated the matter and discovered fraud on the part of the boy concerned, who claimed that Darrell had instructed him in detail. Darrell and his colleague, a minister named George More, still asserting their innocence, ended up in prison, their careers as exorcists at an end. One result of this case was that in 1603 the clergy in general lost the age-old right of exorcism, without the direct authorization of a bishop.

Samuel Harsnett, who later became Archbishop of York, was among those who were appointed to investigate the whole series of exorcisms conducted by John Darrell, and he found so much corruption, falsehood and trickery that he became an outspoken enemy of the witch-hunter, like Reginald Scot before him. Scot's *Discovery of Witchcraft*, published in 1584, was nothing less than an all-out attack on the 'delusion' of witchcraft; Harsnett thoroughly exposed John Darrell in his book *Discovery of the Fraudulent Practices of John Darrell* (1599).

Another interesting case involving John Darrell occurred in 1596 at Burton-on-Trent, in Staffordshire. It concerned a 14-year-old boy, Thomas Darling, who, according to reports, had fits, vomited and claimed to see angels and cats – all green in colour. The local apothecary seemed to be completely puzzled by the case and unable to do anything for the boy. Quite unintentionally, witchcraft was suspected when the reading of a chapter of the Bible coincided with the boy's having convulsions.

A woman living nearby, Alse Gooderidge, who had long been regarded as a witch by the local people, was suspected and when she was confronted by Thomas, he immediately began to have a series of fits – thirty-seven consecutively, according to contemporary reports. The woman Gooderidge was arrested, charged and condemned to death for witchcraft but conveniently died in prison before the sentence could be carried out.

Thomas Darling, still seemingly troubled by fits at all hours of the day and night and in the presence of all manner of persons, turned to John Darrell, who prayed continuously over the boy and apparently exorcized him successfully.

This case and that concerning William Somers were, as we have seen, the downfall of John Darrell as an exorcist, but before we leave him there was another case in which he was called in, involving two young children who seemed to be suffering from demons and devils that continuously possessed them. Here again Darrell was the last resort. A travelling conjuror or 'wise man' had worked wonders with his charms and herbs for a while, but after the travelling man had an argument with the children's parents over payment, the children's fits conveniently began again and spread to other children and to some servants, who all suffered a virtual non-stop outbreak of fits, vomiting, involuntary shouting and barking like dogs.

In the climate of the time and among the people he annoyed, the travelling conjuror had no chance. He was charged with witchcraft and eventually hanged. But the children and the affected adults continued to be troubled by fits and other disturbances, and the seven children and seven adults were all put in the hands of Darrell, who conducted a remarkable and extended exorcism. In fact this exorcism took three whole days and included fasting and interminable prayers, but eventually the demons fled and Darrell had achieved his most spectacular success.

The next, and last, exorcism conducted by Darrell involved an adolescent boy who had seemed impervious to exorcism: during one he had loudly accused three women of bewitching him. Once again Darrell was successful where others had failed but it was a time of suspicion everywhere. William Somers admitted that his possession was a fraud and that he had invented the devils.

Interesting from another point of view is the story of Jane Wenham, who had the distinction of being the last woman upon whom sentence of death was passed for being a witch. This was in 1712, in the village of Walkern in Hertfordshire, and the jury returned a verdict of 'Guilty', in spite of being directed by the justice, Sir John Powell, to acquit the prisoner.

From a review of the evidence, it seems likely that Jane Wenham was a 'cunning woman', a 'conjuror' or a 'white witch', versed in weather lore, well informed on the subject of magical herbs and knowledgeable beyond her time on the power of suggestion. Be that as it may, following the deaths of some of his cattle in what he thought were mysterious circumstances, a farmer, believing that Jane Wenham had bewitched his cattle, called her names. She applied for a warrant against him for slander. The affair seemed to be getting out of hand when the local parson stepped in, hoping to settle the matter amicably.

After hearing both sides, he reproved the farmer for his behaviour and ordered him to pay Jane Wenham one shilling compensation, but Jane was far from happy and declared her dissatisfaction in no uncertain terms. 'If I cannot have justice here,' she said. 'I will have it elsewhere.' These were dangerous words at the time and were to be remembered when shortly afterwards, one of the clergyman's servants fell ill with strange visions. Ann Thorn became convinced that Jane Wenham had bewitched her and said she was constantly troubled by the appearance of cats (one of which bore Jane Wenham's face), and the girl declared that she was being urged to commit suicide.

Jane Wenham was searched for witches' marks, was pricked with long needles and underwent cruel and disgraceful 'examination', but without success for the examiners. Then she was subjected to the Lord's Prayer test and – success at last – she did not seem able to recite 'Forgive us our trespasses' or 'Lead us not into temptation'. Dispite her protestations of innocence, she was indicted as a witch. She submitted to an exhaustive exorcism; without success.

Soon a 'confession' was obtained from her. She admitted that she had bewitched the clergyman's servant (who was still suffering fits) and she named others who had been her assistants. A 'witch bottle' containing urine, hair and nail clippings burst when placed on a fire and when some 'cakes of feathers', said to have been discovered under the pillow of the sick girl, were burned, she experienced relief from her sufferings. Now nothing could save Jane.

After her sentence the judge managed to delay the execution, and then he secured a royal pardon for the 'wise woman' but such a public outcry followed that her life was in danger and she was removed to a place of safety by two convinced disbelievers in witchcraft. The squire of Gilston provided her with a cottage, and she received a small pension for life.

What is interesting is the fate of the 'bewitched' girl. After Jane had 'disappeared', the girl still vomited pins and needles, suffered fits and saw visions. It was suggested by a physician that she wash her hands and face twice a day; he gave instructions that she be kept under observation, day and night, and shrewdly he recommended 'a lusty young fellow' for this particular task. Sure enough, the fits and vomiting and visions ceased and before long Ann married her 'lusty' attendant and custodian. Perhaps that was a form of exorcism. In any case, as far as witchcraft was concerned, the age of reason was at last dawning.

Exorcists always had to be careful how they acted or they could easily find themselves in trouble. A case in point is the eighteenth-century Edmund Hartley who, having made something of a name for himself with popish charms, herbs and incantations, was called in to deal with several children who claimed to be possessed of little devils and certainly acted as though this were the case. Hartley carried out his exorcisms, which had some singular and unusual aspects, and, pronouncing the children cleansed, proceeded to try to over-charge the parents. The Church was consulted and said Hartley had practised witchcraft and he was promptly put on trial. He boasted that the court could not hang him, since the transgression of which he was accused was his first offence, but it was revealed that he had once made a magic circle and because of this he was indeed hanged, on a charge of witchcraft. The children all promptly recovered.

Meanwhile in Spain, to mention one European country where witchcraft was rife, the methods and practices of such people as the brutal witch-hunter Pierre de Lancre surprise and shock us to this day. I have talked with Julio Caro Baroja, whom I have already mentioned, and he told me that he spent the formative years of his life in the Basque provinces and in those days many of the local people still believed in magic and witchcraft.

As a young man he talked with elderly people born in the 1850s who were utterly convinced that there really were men and women who could change themselves into animals, who could fly through the air and do other things which, '... for want of a better word, we generally call witchcraft'. I remember (we met in Spain some years ago) that he said it was all too easy to criticize the inquisitors, the judges and others who dealt with witchcraft in the nineteenth century, but it was important to look at the historical background in which such events took place. In all probability it would be found that the activities of the sorcerers, witches and enchanters were so bound up with the actions of other members of their society that neither they nor their judges could escape the demands of social order: '... which is as much or more an order of social action as of religious or intellectual ideas'.

Yet we know that witchcraft and exorcism are as old as religion, and for that reason, if not for any other, most religions developed special techniques for dealing with the problem of apparent demonic intrusion, infestation or possession.

Primitive means of expelling evil forces, as it was to treat mental disorders, included verbal abuse: shouting, screaming and passionate pleading; physical assault: beating, whipping and the use of torture instruments; and other more subtle approaches: whispering, deprivation of light and sleep, sudden shocks – but the only real effect that any of these techniques had was of virtually scaring to death a few so-called witches. Only very rarely did an assault upon a person's total personality apparently displace psychoneurotic symptoms, but this, in the view of the exorcist, spelled success.

In some cases, and this is obvious from the literature of witchcraft, religious rituals of exorcism made matters worse, enhancing the egomania of the unbalanced individual, so that perverse behaviour became rationalized, self-perpetuating and completely out of control; resulting, in extreme cases, as we have seen, in total psychosis and even murder.

It may be that exorcism can only fully succeed when those who feel that they are or appear to be suffering from the effect of evil forces are able to discover a wider and deeper meaning to life than the mundane existence we all know; this in turn enables them to see witchcraft as the squalid pretension it frequently turns out to be.

Dom Robert Petitpierre, the Benedictine exorcist, once told me that he believed there were *at least* 40,000 self-proclaiming witches and black magicians practising in Britain today; David Marriott, a former Methodist and one-time black magician, said in 1983 that he believed that more than 200,000 people in Britain were, or thought they were, in contact with evil forces. This figure may be exaggerated, but it cannot but be odd that so many believe in 'evil forces' when the existence of the Devil, according to repeated polls and surveys, is denied by the vast majority of the population.

Sybil Leek, the celebrated and self-confessed witch who lived for years with gypsies in the New Forest, told me that occult forces could be used 'for good, as in witchcraft, or for destructive purposes, as in black magic'. She maintained that 'the dark forces of black magic' were gathering in this day and age at a much greater rate that at any time since the Middle Ages; and they may be better organized – so David Marriott may be right.

As Leigh Hunt (1784–1859), the esssayist and poet, points out in one of his essays, 'Before the devil's existence was denied people began to perceive that considerable doubt might be entertained as to the extent of his operations and how far King James and others had a right to palm upon him the offences of their "corrupted flesh".' In his book *Demonologie* (1597) the King says that those who deny the power of a devil would likewise deny the power of God – and that is a sobering thought in this godless age!

Robert Herrick (1591–1674), the poet son of a rich goldsmith and friend of 'rare' Ben Jonson – Herrick's lyrics included 'Cherry Ripe' and 'Gather ye Rosebuds' – took a cynical view of exorcism, and let us end this chapter on exorcism and witchcraft with his satirical view of the subject:

> Holy water come and bring,
> Cat in salt for seasoning,
> Set the brush for sprinkling;
> Sacred spittle bring ye hither,
> Meal and it now mix together,
> And a little oil to either.
> Give the tapers here their light,
> Ring the saints' bell to affright
> Far from hence the evil sprite ...

6 Exorcism and Vampires

When vampires come into the conversation, credibility flies out of the window – or does it? My book *The Vampire's Bedside Companion* resulted in a great many letters from readers asking (in the words of one of my chapters) 'Can Such Things Be?' I usually replied by pointing out that the Hon. Ralph Shirley[1] told me in the 1940s that he had studied the subject in some depth, sifted the evidence and concluded that vampirism was by no means as dead as many people supposed; more likely, he thought, the facts were concealed in the same way as the birth of monsters was for many years.

The idea of vampirism is in fact based on one of the earliest supernatural legends in the world, and the historical overlapping cannot but have contributed to the lasting prevalence of the legend – if legend it is – for the two Christian Churches, the Catholic and the Orthodox, have completely opposing views on the fate of the good and of the bad, after death. The Catholic Church has always held that the bodies of the saints do not decay, while the Orthodox Church maintains that the bodies of the wicked do not decay – they are so bad that the earth itself refuses to take them back to its bosom.

While some writers on the subject of vampirism have ascribed the origin of the belief in such creatures to Greek Christianity, there are in fact traces of the 'superstition' and 'belief' at a considerably earlier date, and no less an authority on the subject than my old friend Montague Summers has, to his own satisfaction at least, traced back 'the dark tradition of the vampire' until it is 'lost amid the ages of a dateless antiquity'.

And as long as there has been belief in vampires there have been special methods of exorcism decreed for dealing with 'the undead'. In Transylvania, one of the ancient homes of the belief, it was thought that every person killed by a vampire became in turn a vampire and continued to suck the blood of other innocent people until the 'evil spirit' was exorcized, and this was done either by opening the grave of the suspected vampire and driving a stake through the corpse or by firing a pistol into the coffin. In obstinate cases it was recommended to cut off the head, fill the mouth with garlic and then replace the head in its proper place in the coffin; alternatively the head could be extracted and burned and the ashes strewn over the grave of the vampire.

At one time the Greek Church taught that bodies of persons upon whom the ban of excommunication had been passed did not undergo decomposition after death, until such sentence had been revoked by the pronouncement of absolution over the remains and, an important point for those who believed in vampirism, while the bodies remained in this uncorrupted condition, the 'spirits' of these unhappy individuals could wander abroad seeking sustenance from the blood of the living.

When theologians were asked about the non-corruption of the body's being one of the proofs of sanctity, they replied that in those cases the body preserved its natural colour and exuded an agreeable odour, whereas the bodies of the excommunicated generally turned black, swelled up and emitted an offensive smell.

Those in authority were still in difficulties, however, for very frequently, it was said, when the graves of suspected vampires were opened, the faces and bodies were found to be pink and healthy-looking, the veins distended with blood, so that, when pierced, they produced a plentiful supply of blood, as fresh and as free as that to be found in the veins of young and healthy living persons.

The teachings were amended and became confused; even more so when it was stated that the bodies of murderers and suicides were also 'exempt from the law of dissolution' until granted release by the Church, and this assumption by the priests of power over the body as well as over the soul only added to the widening belief in vampires.

There is the story of St Libentius, Archbishop of Bremen (d.1013), excommunicating a gang of pirates, one of whom died shortly afterwards and was buried in Norway. Seventy years later his body was found to be 'quite entire and uncorrupted'; '... nor did it fall to dust until it had received absolution from the Bishop Alvareda'. Such is the power of exorcism.

There is also the story related concerning the Court of Mohammed II (1430–81), Sultan of Turkey. A number of learned men investigated a variety of points concerning the Christian faith and informed the Sultan that the bodies of persons excommunicated by the Christian clergy did not decompose. When the Sultan asked whether exorcism or absolution dissolved the bodies, he was told that it did.

Puzzled by this curious information, the Sultan sent orders to Maximus, the Patriarch or bishop, head of the Eastern Church at the time, to produce a case whereby the truth of the matter might be tested.

Maximus convened his clergy in some trepidation, but after lengthy enquiries and deliberation he ascertained that a certain woman had been excommunicated by the previous Patriarch for the commission of grievous sin. The whereabouts of her grave was ascertained, and when it was discreetly opened the corpse was found to be whole and undecomposed but much swollen. When this news was communicated to the Sultan, he immediately despatched a party of men to retrieve the body, in its coffin, which they did.

On an appointed day the liturgy was said over it, the Patriarch recited the absolution, and a ritual of exorcism was recited, in the presence of Court officials who had seen the body intact. As the rites were completed, the bones in the long-dead body were heard to rattle as they fell apart inside the coffin, and at least one of those present maintained that the woman's soul was freed and escaped from the coffin to which it had been condemned.

The Sultan, when he heard of the event, was astonished and exclaimed: 'Of a surety the Christian religion must be true!' Further enquiries, according to the story, revealed that the body had been entirely black, as well as being much swollen; that after being scrutinized the coffin had been sealed with the Sultan's seal and that, three days after the exorcism and absolution had been performed, the coffin was opened and found to contain nothing but dust.

In a nineteenth-century treatise on the Greek and Armenian Churches (Rycaut's *The Present State of the Greek and Armenian Churches*), the author relates a story originating from a preacher named Safronio, 'a person of no mean repute and learning'. It seems that a certain person, for some unspecified misdemeanours, fled to a small island where he escaped the hand of

justice, but he could not avoid the sentence of excommunication. In due course he died, the sentence of the Church
never having been revoked; and when it was realized that this
was an excommunicated man, his body was interred without
any religious ceremony in unconsecrated ground. Before long
the relatives of the deceased became anxious and worried about
the increasing stories from local people in the vicinity of the
burial place of disturbances and frightening appearances at
night-time, when a strange and unusual apparition arose from
the grave, they asserted, of the 'accursed excommunicant'.

Soon, in accordance with custom in these circumstances, the
local people disinterred the coffin and opened it. They found the
body uncorrupted, ruddy even, and the veins replete with
blood. They furnished the coffin with grapes, apples, nuts and
such fruit as the season afforded and then reburied the body.
Some of them had wanted to resort to more extreme remedies
that were recommended in such cases, such as cutting the body
into several parts and boiling it in wines, an approved method of
dislodging an evil spirit and disposing the body to dissolution.
The friends and relatives of the dead man, wishing the corpse to
rest in peace and believing that the provision of fruit and nuts
would ease the departed soul, argued against more extreme
measures, and they obtained a reprieve from the clergy – on the
handing over of a sum of money, on the clear understanding
that a release from excommunication would be obtained.

Accordingly the necessary arrangements were made, and
letters of authority have been preserved to this day. It was
expressly stated that, should the Patriarch in Constantinople
condescend to make the ritual that was necessary to remove the
excommunication, the day, the hour and the minute of the
remission should be carefully noted and inserted into the
appropriate document.

Meanwhile the corpse had been taken into a church in the
vicinity of its burial-place, prayers and Masses were said for its
dissolution and for the pardon of the offender day after day, and
then, after many prayers, supplications and offerings and
exorcisms, and while Sofronio himself was performing divine
service one day, there was heard a sudden rumbling noise from
the coffin of the dead man, much to the fear of those present.

After the service Sofronio and other clergy opened the coffin
and found the body utterly consumed and dissolved as if it had

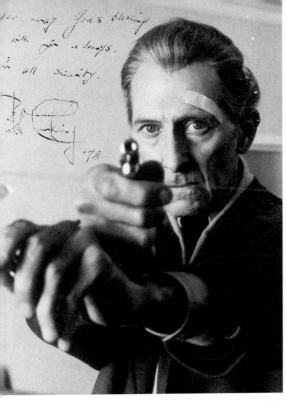

Exorcism of a vampire!
The popular conception
as portrayed by actor
Peter Cushing

Robert Aickmann (1914–1981), the distinguished writer of
strange tales, had an immense knowledge of the occult and once
exorcized a vampire in Venice

The vicar and his wife outside their haunted Berkshire church and vicarage, both of which were subjected to exorcism in 1982

Highgate Cemetery: a photograph taken at the time of the hunt for the Highgate vampire

Sean Manchester, at the time of the Highgate exorcism, with some of the accoutrements of the vampire-hunter: crucifixes, garlic and wooden stakes

The haunted church at Langenhoe, Essex, where attempts at exorcism seemed only to induce psychic activity

Inset: The somewhat mysterious Rev. Montague Summers (1880–1948), who claimed to have exorcized many ghosts and vampires. The Rev. Donald Omand exorcizing the evil from Loch Ness

Conrad Veidt (1893–1943), the German-born stage and screen actor, who 'exorcized' the ghosts that haunted his London home

The Lee Penny – allegedly
used in exorcisms for
many centuries

The trial of a pig at
Lausanne in the
fourteenth century: the
frontispiece to a book
entitled *Credulities, Past
and Present* by William
Jones FSA, published in
1880

Canon John D. Pearce-Higgins, Vice-Provost of Southwark Cathedral, who carried out dozens of exorcisms with and without the help of mediums

Below: Marelands, Bentley, Hants. Here there are conflicting stories of ghosts and a 'haunted room', in which an extended service of exorcism was considered necessary

St Vitus exorcizing a demon which is making for the window! A painting by Michael Walgemut (*c.* 1540) in the German National Museum, Nuremberg

Horace Walpole's silver bell, attributed to Benvenuto Cellini and thought to have been manufactured and used for the cursing, excommunication and exorcism of animals

been interred several years previously. The hour and minute of this dissolution were immediately and most carefully noted and were found to compare precisely with the date, the hour and indeed the minute of the Patriarch's service of release in Constantinople. At the moment of release the body had turned to dust.

Advancing to 1844, we find M. Cyprien Robert, Professor of Slavonic Letters and Literature at the Collège de France, describing some of the 'dark traditions of unhappy souls' in Serbia and Herzogovina who, after death, are '… condemned to wander hither and thither over the earth to expiate their sins, or live a horrid life in death in the tomb as vampires …'

M. Robert refers to the exorcizing of the vampire: 'When a dead man is suspected of leaving his place of sepulture, the corpse is solemnly exhumed; if it be in a state of putrefaction and decay then the priest will sprinkle it with holy water; if it be ruddy and fresh-complexioned it is exorcized, and placed in the earth again, where before it is covered a sharp stake is thrust through and through the carcass lest it stir forth once more. Not long since it was customary among the Serbians to riddle the head of the corpse with their bullets and then to burn it entire. This is seldom done now, but they firmly believe that even the carrion crow will shun the living corpse, and wing fast away from such ill-omened flesh.'

And coming up to the present day we have Dr Devandra P. Varma, Professor of English at Dalhousie University, Halifax, Nova Scotia, in a letter to me dated 18 January 1974, asserting 'I believe in vampires and I have proofs …' After subsequent correspondence and meeting with Dr Varma when he lectured at the Ghost Club in 1987, I am in no doubt that this much-travelled, erudite and experienced explorer of the strange and the unusual has indeed come to accept beyond question the real and actual existence of vampires.

'The vampire is not a ghostly figure appearing like a demon from hell with fangs bared and eyes bloodied,' Dr Varma will tell you. 'He is tall and handsome, his hair dark and well-groomed; despite the waxen pallor of his face and hands, he has flashing dark eyes and a vivid redness in his lips that are curled in a smile. As the undead he casts no shadow and has no reflection, but what is prominent are his canine teeth.

'The hollow beneath his eyes adds to his romantic expression of undefinable melancholy diffusing a lonesome sadness. His black cloak flutters in the breeze as he silently glides along empty corridors while the wind rustles thorough shroudlike ghostly curtains ...'

Can such things *really* be? Let us listen to Dr Varma again for a moment, for he entertains no doubts. 'The concept of the dead arising from their graves to feed upon the blood of the innocent and the beautiful is not a macabre but a voluptuous idea,' he told me quietly in the peaceful solace of a famous London club. 'The vampire works out his spell in the dark ... he rises from the moist and damp earth in a glowing mist or black fog from the vaults that rest under cobwebs in the faint light of the dim radiance of a rising moon ...'

Earlier he had told Ghost Club members of his visits to the 'land beyond the Forest', that 'remote and forgotten corner of the world', 'the wilds of Transylvania' where, to this day, we were told, 'stalk creatures of the dark'. Here they still drive stakes through the dead bodies of people they are convinced are vampires and they still hang garlic blossoms above the doorways: '... for vampires exorcism is the only salvation'.

Many curious examples of apparent vampirism and lycanthropy have been preserved through the years, and services of exorcism that have apparently released these awful beings; both the original accounts and the elaborate exorcisms remain to puzzle us to this day. There is, for example, John Cuthbert Lawson's evidence[2] relating to excavations that were carried out in Cyprus under the auspices of the British Museum in the spring of 1899.

The directors of the operation heard several stories from different members of their workforce concerning the detection of a vampire-like creature and of its exorcism and disappearance. It seemed that in one particular village the inhabitants had suffered from the ravages of a nocturnal marauder, whom they suspected of being a vampire.

A party of local men armed themselves not only with weapons but also with crucifixes, stakes and holy water, and they kept watch, night after night. At length, one moonlit evening some of them espied what looked like a vampire; certainly he was acting suspiciously. Before they really had time to decide what to do, one of the company fired a shot and apparently succeeded in wounding the monstrous being, which, however, escaped from the trap they had hastily prepared and sped away into the darkness.

Next day it was observed that a certain man in the village, who had not been among the party hunting the vampire the night before, was marked with an injury which exactly corresponded with the wound inflicted on the vampire. During subsequent interrogation the unfortunate individual confessed that he was indeed a vampire and was the nocturnal visitor they had been seeking. What then happened in this particular case is not recorded but it seems that attempts at exorcism of the victim who admitted being a vampire and precautions against visitations of the vampire were unsuccessful.

Perhaps they should have tried the Vampire Protection Medallion, which may or may not be a genuine fifteenth-century object; in all probability it is what is known as a 'Billie and Charlie'. These curious objects are more properly known as 'Shadwell Dock forgeries'.

Apparently these concoctions first came to light in 1858 during excavation for the new Shadwell Dock in East London, and there were numerous varieties depicting daggers, knights, ecclesiastical symbols and triptychs. The one now in my possession is a heavy brass medallion decorated on one side with a figure armed with a sword and a stake, and on the other side there is the mail-clad head of a man with a long nose and staring eyes, a flaming brand and a cross with a circle over it, the whole being surmounted by two sharp-beaked birds with their heads turned outwards.

These objects, I have been told by a well-known coin-dealer, created considerable controversy in the antiquarian and archaeological worlds at the time they first appeared, and many theories were put forward as to their historical significance and authenticity.

Some time later two men, William Smith and Charles Eaton ('Billie' and 'Charlie'), residing at the time in Rosemary Lane, Tower Hill, were found to be in possession of the moulds and implements required for the mauufacture of the medallions, and prosecutions took place. The men were employed at Shadwell Dock as mud-rakers and had made and then deposited the forgeries, only to 'find' them later and sell them as objects of antiquity. A few years ago Mr J. Webb of Dolphin Coins told me that his firm had a fairly extensive collection of such places, some depicting scenes of a sacrificial nature and others quasi-sacrificial implements. He added that the legends around the medallions are quite meaningless, Messrs Smith and Eaton being totally illiterate!

Be that as it may, Montague Summers, from whom I obtained my medallion, was a convinced believer in the very real existence of vampires, and he certainly believed in the efficacy of this particular 'Vampire Protection Medallion', which he told me he had proved beyond any shadow of a doubt, not once but a score of times.

The story of how the somewhat mysterious medallion came into my possession is interesting, since it concerns my involvement in and investigation of an apparent vampire infestation.

I may say that I owe much of my interest in vampirism to Montague Summers, who told me many stories of vampire infestation, some of which he had personally investigated, including two in Greece, where he lived in 1906 and 1907.

Once, he told me, he recited the words of absolution over the body of a young woman whom the villagers said was a vampire; just before they drove a stake through her heart, as he came to the end of the 'exorcism', the body, which had been dead for many years but seemed to be completely preserved, suddenly shrank and twisted and snarled as though trying to get away from the holy words. He was so terrified that he left the graveside, but he never forgot the awful shriek as the stake was hammered home, and when he went back to the graveside, all that remained in the coffin was a mass of foul-smelling dust.

It was Summers too who first told me of a Russian vampire, a story that I believe he obtained from Professor Paul Ariste of Tartu University. It concerned a girl who met a young man in a forest. After a time the couple fell in love, but the young man's parents, when they heard of the affair, forbade their son to see the girl again, for she was poor and, they thought, quite unsuitable for their only son. For a time the couple met in secret, but then they were discovered and the son was watched day and night. He pined and longed for his love and before long he refused to eat or drink if he could not see her, but still the family did not relent. Too late they realized that he was ill, and soon the boy died.

The girl knew nothing of what had happened, and one night

the boy appeared to her in her bedroom and beckoned her to follow him. She rose from her bed and followed her lover. He led her to the churchyard, showed her an empty coffin and motioned her to lie in it as her bed. As she prepared to do so, a cock crowed and the young man fell into the coffin on top of her as though dead.

In her anguish the girl hastened to the local priest and told him everything that had happened. He knew the man she spoke of was dead, for he had buried him. Early next morning he went to the churchyard and took the coffin containing the boy's body into the church. That night he arranged for the girl and a number of other maidens from the village to gather in the church; all the girls were dressed alike, for the priest wanted the ghost, if it walked, to be puzzled and confused as to which one was his lover, so that the priest would have time to do what he knew was necessary.

Just before midnight the priest and all the girls saw the lid of the coffin lift, a hand appeared, the lid was thrown back and the young man rose up, saw the maidens, spotted his lover and made to take her to his coffin. The priest quickly picked up a Bible and faced him; the young man – or was it his ghost? – let go of the girl, shrank from the Bible, stumbled back to the coffin and fell in. The priest hurried forward, held a crucifix before the staring eyes of the 'corpse' and quickly cut his throat: blood spurted out as from a living man, but the ghost or the vampire was exorcized and never walked again.

Many years ago now I became intrigued by the possibility that vampires really might exist. It all began when I was asked to investigate a case of haunting; little did I think at the time that it would lead me to Montague Summers and to the possession of what is, perhaps, the only vampire medallion in the world.

The people intimately concerned with the haunting were a small family consisting of a widowed mother and her son, a boy of ten; it was the boy who was 'haunted' and seemed to be plagued by a vampire. At first I thought it was a case of poltergeist infestation, for I learned that scores of articles had been moved, strange noises had been heard and seemingly pointless incidents had taken place, but then I learned that only the boy was really involved. It was he who heard the tappings at the window, he who complained of dark shapes appearing in his bedroom at night, and it was only in his room that articles were moved – and it was religious articles such as a crucifix, a Bible and holy pictures that were displaced. The pictures would fall off the walls when the window-tappings started, and they always fell face downwards; the crucifix which the boy's mother used to hang over his bed would swing by itself and rattle and disturb the boy so that he used to take it down and put it on a bedside table, and *always* – at least a score of times, I was told – the crucifix would 'fall' to the floor and somehow make its way right under the bed, or somewhere completely out of sight.

The Bible, if it was left open, would quiver and the pages would turn by themselves, apparently keeping time with the tapping at the window, until the boy would close the book, and then it seemed to stick to his fingers like a magnet, and he found himself moving the book away from the bed. The only way he seemed to be able to release his fingers was to put the Bible right out of sight – then it felt just like an ordinary book again, so he would put it under the bedclothes and leave it there, or put it inside the bedside cabinet or lay it far under the bed. He told me it was very strange to feel it stick tight to his open palm all the time he was looking at it and then, when it was out of sight, fall away immediately. He always thought he must be dreaming, but it happened many times and, like the crucifix and the holy pictures, the Bible would always be out of sight in the morning – after he had had one of his dreams and was feeling drained.

He told me that the strange happenings began soon after his father died. Oddly enough, but in keeping with the vampire tradition, I discovered that his father had, in fact, committed suicide.

That first night the boy had been asleep (or was still asleep, he did not know which) when he found himself disturbed by a tapping noise, and then a sharp 'bang' had woken him up. At that time his mother had not given him the crucifix or left the Bible beside his bed but, he discovered in the morning, the only holy picture then in the room had fallen onto its face during the night. The glass was broken but the picture wire was intact and the hook was still firmly fixed in the wall.

As he snuggled down to go back to sleep after starting up at the loud 'bang', he saw the dark sky and bright stars through the window, and then they were blotted out by 'something black' that seemed to quiver outside the window. He heard a light but persistent tapping, and he thought he saw a pair of red eyes looking in at him. He screamed and his mother came in and comforted him. She drew the curtains and stayed with him until he was sleeping peacefully again – which, she told me, was not until dawn was breaking, when she heard a cock crowing.

A few nights later the boy again found himself awakened by various noises in his bedroom. First a single 'crash' which later proved to have been caused by the falling – or jumping – of the holy picture, which again lay on its face; then a rhythmic clinking noise which originated from the crucifix which his mother had hung on the bed-rail over his head, and by a light tapping noise that came from the direction of the half-curtained window.

Thinking that his turning in the bed had set the crucifix swinging, which it continued to do as he lay still in bed, the boy reached up and removed it (he told me that it felt warm), placing it, as he thought, on the bed-table nearby, although in the morning it was found far under the bed, face-down and deeply scratched across the back. The boy's mother insisted that the crucifix had been unmarked when she had hung it in her son's room, and certainly the marks looked very recent. The cut was diagonally across the crucifix and, I would have thought, could have been made only by a heavy instrument, machinery or enormous strength.

Having removed the crucifix, the boy looked towards the window, and as he looked, the tapping noise ceased. He told me that something like black smoke seemed to pour into the room through one of the small upper windows which had been left open for air, and then, as he watched, the smoke gathered itself into a more or less solid shape and began to come towards him. He said he was just about to scream when he seemed to be enveloped in blackness, and he knew no more until next morning, when his mother found him pale and listless, with no mark on him. She put his condition down to a restless night and bad dreams following the death of his father.

For a few days the boy slept in another room, where he was undisturbed, but after he had returned to his own room for about a week, the same thing happened again, and it was then that they sought the help of a priest, who suggested a doctor, who brought me into the affair.

As it was my first case of vampirism – if vampirism it was – I wrote to Montague Summers and we exchanged several letters.

He suggested a complicated idea for catching the vampire, with the boy as bait, and then dealing with it in the usual fashion of vampires, but the boy's mother was horrified at the idea and instead obtained holy water and had the room blessed by the priest. She hung two more holy pictures in the room, and for a few weeks all was quiet. Then I had a frantic call from the mother to come and see what had happened.

I found the boy in bed in another room to which he had been taken. He seemed really ill, terribly weak and listless, with hardly enough strength to tell me what had happened, although the doctor had been and given him something, so perhaps his condition when I saw him was due partly to sedation. Then I saw the bedroom where he had spent the night, and if I had previous doubts about vampires, they soon disappeared when I entered that room.

The window was smashed and glass littered the floor: it had been smashed from the outside. One holy picture was facing the wall, its wire twisted so tightly, where the picture had been turned round and round again and again, that eventually it had to be cut from the wall – the wire was literally squeezed together as though with metal pliers, used with great strength. Two other holy pictures lay face down on the floor, their cords and hooks intact. The heavy crucifix lay on its face by the far wall, buckled and bent until it was hardly recognizable, and above it there was a deep indentation where it had struck the wall – it must have been thrown with considerable force. The Bible was underneath the bed, drenched with some abominable matter so that every page had stuck together. And the smell in the room was absolutely foul.

I hastened to Montague Summers, and it was then that he brought out for my inspection the curious heavy brass medallion which, I was told, was a fifteenth-century mid-European medallion that had proved its power a score of times over the years as a protection against vampires. He related to me some of the many times that the medallion had been used, always with success, and then, somewhat to my astonishment, he pressed the medal into my hand and said, 'You keep it.'

I thought he meant to use it in the case in hand, and we talked about that again, and then he picked up the medallion and weighed it in his hand. He said he believed that it was probably the most effective talisman in existence against vampires – and evil spirits – and he blessed it for me and told me to keep it always. He was sure that I would have occasion to use it many times, for he was quite convinced that there were vampires everywhere, but he warned me that its effectiveness would deteriorate if its power was publicized, so he urged me to say nothing about it to anyone and always to keep it in the dark.

Well, all that was over a quarter of a century ago, and I have never been called upon to use it since, so perhaps he will forgive me for writing about it now. There may be people troubled by vampires whom I can help, but I doubt it somehow.

I made a point of taking the medallion with me when next I went to see how things were progressing with the 'vampire-haunted boy', but I never used it. The doctor had prescribed a change of climate for the boy, different surroundings and, if possible, a trip abroad. Already his mother had arranged to visit her married sister in South Africa, and soon afterwards they left. As far as I know, they never returned to Britain and had no more trouble with vampires. At least they promised to let me know if they did, and I never heard any more from them. If they should chance to read this account, I hope they will not take exception to anything I have said. I would be very interested to hear from them again.

I have the 'vampire protection' medallion in front of me as I write. Has it really been used against vampires, as Montague Summers asserted, or is it a 'Billie and Charlie'? Too late to ask Montague Summers now; he died over forty years ago. On 26 November 1988 a memorial stone was erected over his previously unmarked grave in Richmond Cemetery, Surrey.

Another man I knew, with a great interest in vampires, was Robert Fordyce Aickman (1914–81), a widely recognized and distinguished writer of strange tales who had 'an immense knowledge of the occult' (*The Times*) based on many years study and practical investigation.

He once told me that he had no doubt at all that there had once been vampires but he doubted whether they existed today – although he could not be sure. After a talk at the Ghost Club some years ago by a man who claimed to have had first-hand encounters with vampires and showed photographs to 'prove' it, Robert observed to me, 'Most interesting talk – but I don't believe a word of it.'

He told me that he had met a man in Venice who he believed was a vampire. He had learned what he could of the man without raising too much suspicion, and there seemed to be good evidence that the man was extremely aged, although he appeared to be at the prime of his life, in early middle age, and as fit and strong as any man Robert had ever met.

A young girl who was accompanying Robert became 'enamoured' of this strange man, who purported to be in Venice on a visit from Eastern Europe. When she became completely besotted with the man, Robert consulted a Viennese doctor he knew who was knowledgeable on vampiric conditions. He was persuaded to join Robert in Venice, and as soon as he met the virile, dark-eyed stranger, he too felt convinced that the man was indeed a vampire.

Robert and the doctor made their plans in secret, and one night they trapped the man they believed was a vampire in the girl's bedroom, having ensured that she was safely elsewhere. There they both faced the man, who glared at the crucifixes they suddenly produced and carried in front of them, preventing his escape by the only door. He turned and made for the window, only to find garlic surrounding it – suddenly at bay, he seemed to charge straight at Robert, who called upon all his religious faith for deliverance from the vampire facing him, and the next moment there was no one in the room except Robert and the doctor, apart from a thick grey mist that seeped past the would-be exorcists and disappeared under the closed door.

They left Venice the next day, with the girl, and none of them ever saw the man again, although Robert was completely convinced for the rest of his life that he had been instrumental in saving the girl from a vampire. When I spoke to her, she supported Robert and his story in every particular.

Another man, also well versed in all supernatural and occult subjects and who believed in vampires – he told me that he had 'undoubtedly' met several, was Algernon Blackwood. I have written elsewhere[3] that '...one of the memorable pleasures of the Ghost Club some years go was the likelihood of an encounter with Algernon Blackwood (1869–1951), a charming raconteur with a commanding presence, an unforgettable face and an enormous knowledge of the occult. A son of Sir Arthur Blackwood and Sidney, Duchess of Manchester, he went to Canada when he was twenty, where a wide variety of jobs in different locales provided him with background information for his many weird stories.'

A dedicated explorer of the occult and an associate of W.B. Yeats (another Ghost Club member), Blackwood told me that his vampire story *The Transfer* is nearer to truth than he cared to remember. There really had been an original of the man he called 'Mr Frene, senior' with a 'hard, bleak face ... very thin ... and with curious, oily, bright and steady eyes that did not glitter, but drew you with a sort of soft, creamy shine like Eastern eyes ... he dominated us all, yet so gently that until it was accomplished no one noticed it ...' That strange man with the 'enormous' face, who had transferred vitality and life from others to himself for years, had really existed. And there really had been a patch of garden where for years nothing grew, the Forbidden Corner, until, in a curious exorcism that used a child's double, an extraordinary power or 'something' toppled and destroyed the psychic vampire; he had been defeated in that Forbidden Corner and had disappeared, but within months that plot of ground where nothing had ever grown within living memory was 'full of great, luscious, driving weeds and creepers, very strong, full-fed, and bursting thick with life'.

When I was researching *The Vampire's Bedside Companion* in 1974, Sean Manchester, president of the British Occult Society and something of an expert on present-day vampires was kind enough to contribute a chapter[4] and I will paraphrase his remarkable story of the Highgate vampire.

The story really began when two 16-year-old schoolgirls saw what appeared to be dead bodies emerging from graves, when they were walking past Highgate Cemetery one night. Afterwards one of the girls, Elizabeth Wojdyla, began to be troubled by a series of nightmares in which someone or something with a deathly white face was trying to enter her bedroom window.

Two years later Sean Manchester chanced to meet Elizabeth Wojdyla, and he was immediately struck by her appearance. Although she was a charming and intelligent young lady, her features had become cadaverous and her complexion deathly pale: she appeared to be suffering from a pernicious form of anaemia. She now lived on her own in a flat in the Highgate area, and she was still suffering from the nightmares.

Always around midnight, not every night but regularly and

frequently, she became aware of a stillness as she lay almost asleep, and then she had the impression of 'something' approaching her bed. Although she could sense the danger, she was unable to move. She became aware of something with glaring eyes and sharp teeth very close to her; then something would touch her and she would remember nothing more. On one occasion she felt an almost irresistible urge to rise from her bed and go outside in the middle of the night.

A few weeks later Elizabeth Wojdyla's boyfriend telephoned Sean Manchester and said he was very worried. Elizabeth was ill; she ate hardly anything and was so weak she could hardly walk. The doctor had prescribed iron tablets and vitamin pills but they did not seem to be doing her any good at all. Sean Manchester visited the girl and was again struck by the deterioration in her condition; not only had she lost a lot more weight but her face was dull and lifeless, and she appeared to be completely without energy or the will to help herself. When he was shown two inflamed marks on her neck, he no longer had any doubt that he was faced with a case of vampirism.

Three days later Sean Manchester learned that in the middle of the night Elizabeth had risen from her bed and gone out to Highgate Cemetery, where she had been found staring through the iron railings, almost in a state of trance. Later that night her boyfriend had heard a stifled cry from Elizabeth's bedroom and, bursting in, found her gasping for breath, with specks of blood on her pillow.

Sean Manchester lost no further time. The door and window of the girl's bedroom were sealed with garlic and protected by crucifixes. Salt and a silver cross were hung round her neck. Passages from the Bible were placed under her pillow. Holy water was sprinkled about the room, and prayers were recited. A lay exorcism was carried out.

For a week Elizabeth was restless at night and sometimes requested, in a somewhat strained voice, that the antidotes and religious artefacts be removed from her room, for they seemed to stifle and overpower her, but everything was left as Sean Manchester had arranged it, and as the days passed with uneventful nights, the restlessness became less and she began to eat and drink, and her complexion improved considerably. Slowly the small punctures on her neck, bathed with holy water, faded and eventually disappeared. Within a few months

Elizabeth Wojdyla was her happy, normal self; the exorcism proceedings had served their purpose, and all was well.

But Sean Manchester was worried about who else might become a victim to the vampire that had, presumably, caused Elizabeth so much distress, and after a number of other apparent vampire attacks and sightings, he seriously set about investigating the possibility of Highgate Cemetery's harbouring a vampire.

One of the first people with whom he now came in contact was the sister of a beautiful young lady, whom we will call Lusia. Both she and her sister had of late had the impression that they were being suffocated while asleep at night, and they had both experienced what they called 'sleep-walking' in the vicinity of Highgate Cemetery. Sean Manchester then discovered that Lusia had two tiny pin-pricks on her neck! He arranged to be informed immediately if Lusia was again disturbed at night in this way, and twice he was called and saw her staring from the window in the direction of Highgate Cemetery, with a blank expression on her face.

On the third occasion, when he arrived at the sisters' flat, he found a note for him saying that Lusia had gone to the cemetery and that her sister had gone after her. Sean Manchester hurried there himself and discovered the two young ladies in the act of entering Highgate Cemetery through a gap in the railings; Lusia in particular appeared to be in a deep trance.

Deep in the recesses of the quiet cemetery Sean Manchester followed as Lusia and her sister reached the Columbarium (a burial place containing niches for cinerary urns) and there Lusia stopped in front of an iron door. Suddenly she ripped off the crucifix that she wore, and she seemed about to pass into the tomb when Sean Manchester took from his pocket a silver cross and threw it between her and the doorway to the tomb. Lusia stopped in her tracks, gasped and then collapsed in a heap on the ground. She was carried home, more unconscious than conscious, and afterwards she had no memory whatever of the event.

Sean Manchester now knew that he would have to hunt out the vampire and seek to exorcize him. He said at the time that he would like to '... exorcize the vampire by the traditional and approved manner – drive a stake through its heart with one blow just after dawn between Friday and Saturday, then chop off the head with a gravedigger's shovel and burn the remains – but that would be breaking the law'. In the event he led a party of vampire-hunters to the tomb before midnight on the evening of Friday the 13th. The iron door would not open but he knew of another entry to the tomb: through a hole in the roof of the catacombs, and he and two assistants were lowered into the musty, damp and cobwebbed interior of the tomb. There they found three empty coffins which they lined with garlic and protected with crosses. They then concocted a circle of salt around the coffins and sprinkled holy water within the circle. Feeling confident that they had done all they could, they left the tomb.

Shortly after sunrise Sean Manchester slipped back to the tomb: the coffins were just as they had been earlier – empty. He hoped his efforts had been successful but a few months later three schoolgirls discovered a headless body a few yards from the mysterious vault with the iron door, and he decided to re-examine the crypt and the three coffins inside. He found two of the coffins exactly where they had been before, but one was missing.

A few days later Sean Manchester persuaded Lusia to accompany him to the Columbarium in daylight. With three assistants carrying 'the necessary accoutrements', they made their way to the catacombs one bright August afternoon. There, outside the iron door to which she had once been so attracted, he managed to put Lusia into a deep hypnotic trance. Then, at first answering his questions in her normal voice, she suddenly began talking in a deeper and more sinister tone, and she repeated time after time the phrase: 'You should never have come here … you should never have come here …' Asked why, she replied: 'Evil has triumphed over good.'

While she was still in this deep trance, Sean Manchester took her back to the night she had visited this place in a somnambulistic state, and after several unsuccessful attempts she eventually re-enacted the events of that night verbally and in her normal voice. 'Yes, yes,' she said eagerly. 'I'm coming … I'm coming …' Suddenly she started laughing; then she stood up straight and called out, 'Where are you? … Where are you? …' She ran to the iron door and tried to get through. Her cries of 'Where are you?' echoed through the empty catacombs. Suddenly she appeared to give up, and she walked into a nearby empty vault and began sobbing; it was the place where the headless corpse had been discovered. Sean Manchester consoled Lusia and carefully brought her out of the trance.

Then the vampire-hunters began their work in earnest. After considerable trouble they succeeded in opening the iron door of the mysteriously attractive vault. Inside, the shelves were full of decaying coffins. Checking the number with that on the inscription outside, there appeared to be one too many! But which one? At the back of the vault, on the floor, the seekers came upon a coffin in better condition than the rest and bearing no nameplate. Cautiously they opened the lid.

Inside there was a body which appeared to be neither dead or alive. 'It's newly dead,' someone suggested, but the vault was a hundred years old and there had been no recent admissions. Sean Manchester took up the stake of aspen he had brought and placed the point between the seventh and eighth rib on the left side of the body – but his associates were concerned at possible sacrilege and begged him to desist. Was there no other way? He thought for a moment: 'We can try,' he replied, but he knew they must act quickly, for the sun would soon be setting.

Replacing the lid on the coffin, he rested a crucifix upon it and placed vessels containing holy water at the four corners, and bags of salt and garlic inside the vault. He also burned incense at the vault entrance and formed a circle of salt around himself and his companions. Handing a crucifix to each of them, he suggested they all pray in silence, asking for strength to banish 'this evil' for ever. He explained to Lusia that she must remain inside the circle of salt at all times and do exactly as she might be instructed. He then handed her a Bible and opened it at the 54th Psalm.

After a moment he began the ancient rite of exorcism of vampires, but first he sprinkled holy water. He made the sign of the cross between each prayer of invocation, each plea for strength and each adjuration.

'O thou Who dost answer the prayers of Thy humble servants, strengthen these efforts in Thy name to counteract the subtleties and evil mischiefs of him who is the Devil's agent. Cause the forces of darkness to be overcome by the angels of light, for the sake of Jesus Christ our Lord.'

As he began the Latin banishment, it suddenly became very cold, and the white candles burning round the circle flickered as if something had caused a draught. One of the assistants placed a hand upon his shoulder and pointed upwards. The sun was setting. Now Sean Manchester shouted the words of exorcism so that they reverberated off the walls of the vault: 'Go forth, thou deceiver, full of all evil and falsehood, the enemy of virtue, the persecutor of the innocent. Give place, thou wicked one; give place, thou evil one; give place to Christ.'

Instantaneously, those deep, voluminous tombs began to vibrate with low, booming sounds that seemed to draw nearer. Lusia became extremely frightened and dropped the Bible she had been holding. She seemed about to step out of the circle when one of Sean's assistants grabbed her and pulled her back. Dusk seemed to fall very quickly.

Raising his right hand, in which he held a large crucifix, Sean Manchester cried: 'Begone, thou hideous demon, unto thine own place and return no more to plague the children of Almighty God.' He then threw the cross with all his might into the darkness of the vault. There was complete silence. The little party stood surrounded by that stony silence for what seemed a long time, not daring to move.

Finally Sean Manchester felt that it was all over, and he made preparations to leave. Picking up the Bible that Lusia had dropped, he noticed that it had fallen open at the Book of Deuteronomy. His eyes fell on the words: ''Only be sure that thou eat not the blood, for the blood is the life ...' (Chapter 12, verse 23).

Later the entrance to the vault was bricked and cemented up, and since then nothing more has been heard of the Highgate Vampire. Had he finally ridden out history into legend or, as someone once asked, is it that mankind cannot bear too much reality?

7   Exorcism at Haunted Houses, Rectories and Churches

Exorcisms of one kind or another have been performed in haunted houses since time immemorial. In many parts of the world primitive man believed that, especially when death takes place suddenly, the mouth of the dead person must be opened to allow the soul to fly out. This 'soul' often wandered about and visited places known to it in life, and the first place it haunted was its own dwelling. Therefore, on three consecutive nights after burial, the relatives of the deceased, on the very spot where the body had laid, would place a vessel of wine and water and a cake; evidence of the folk-belief in the preservation of the soul's individuality and, to a certain extent, of its continuing earthly needs; prevention being better than cure, the 'soul' was placated. If for some reason any part of this practice was not carried out, the 'soul' of the departed could wander indefinitely, and it was then necessary to exorcize it to put the 'soul' at rest.

At the root of the matter lies belief in the power to transfer a spiritual being from place to place by a ritual act and ritual words. The early Romans carried out their *evocatio*, which might be looked upon as an exorcism of the whole community, while ancient Jewish writings are full of stories of exorcism involving the so-called Prayer of Nabonidus, and Jewish exorcists were credited with forgiveness of sins and consequent healing.

Josephus (37–*c*. 100) makes the claim that Solomon was taught by God the art of exorcism, and in early writings exorcism and healing are frequently confused. Baptism was usually preceded by exorcism in early Christian times, the theory being that the candidate had worshipped heathen gods who were no better than demons, and it was a small step to the exorcism of haunted places with holy water, bell, book and candle.

Modern exorcisms at haunted houses are not so very

145

different. I visited several scenes of haunting with the late Canon John Pearce-Higgins, vice-provost of Southwark Cathedral, and he served on the adjudicating panel that I organized some thirty years ago to investigate psychic activity. Other members of that committee were Sir George Joy, Dr Paul Tabori and the Member of Parliament for South Kensington.

John Pearce-Higgins, a cheerful man with a vivid turn of speech, once told me about a haunted house in the Midlands that he had 'cleared up'. He said he could hardly believe what was happening, for he found himself talking to a ghost. He was really puzzled – and that was unusual for John Pearce-Higgins!

'You say you were prior of the abbey here in Tudor times,' he said somewhat scornfully. 'Your name is not on my list of priors. You were a lay brother only – you and your friend as well?' A mumbled response showed that the shot had gone home. 'You killed poor Annie Williams,' John proceeded. 'And you killed her baby too – your baby ...'

'We had to do it,' responded an arrogant voice.

'Nobody *has* to commit murder,' the canon replied. 'You both seduced the girl. You killed mother and child to save your own skins. You had better leave this place. You are not wanted here. Go at once.'

The owner of the 'haunted' house (built with stones from a ruined abbey) was a widow with three sons, and she had written to Canon Pearce-Higgins to say her house was haunted; there were frightening bangs and bumps in the night, there were knocks on the walls, ghostly footsteps and spine-chilling moans. The canon's response to the widow's appeal was to pack his clerical robes and a portable Communion set and, accompanied by a professional medium, Donald Page, set out for the Midlands.

The house stood on the site of the abbey's rest-house, and John Pearce-Higgins, with the aid of Donald Page's spirit guide, soon discovered that the place was infested with several ghosts. A short Communion service was held after contact was made with the haunting entities, during the course of which the whole story of the haunting and the reason for it came out. It transpired that two evil monks had got hold of a stuttering maidservant, Annie Williams, and one or the other of them had made her pregnant. After the birth of the child they had murdered mother and child; now the house was haunted by the ghosts of the murdered girl, her child, the two murdering monks and also several other earthbound monks.

'Annie was looking for her child's body which the monks had buried,' Canon Pearce-Higgins told me. 'The monks, who were very arrogant, remained on the scene of their crime, unable to progress; and the others were just plain ignorant and had no idea what they should do to go on to the next stage of their "life".'

After the exorcism the canon conducted a short Communion service, and there was then a long silence. The monkish ghosts, the earthbound spirits that had been there for centuries, Pearce-Higgins said, had all fled.

'We may be putting on an act,' he told me once, 'but whatever we are doing, it seems to work.' He always claimed to have 'cleared' a number of houses and at least two vicarages. 'The Churches are to blame for ghosts,' he used to say. 'They teach that when people die they are put in a grave to wait for resurrection, bone, worms and all. But after death, as spirits, they find themselves alive and well.

'I believe, as a Christian, that it is the Church's job to tell earthbound spirits to go on and up and not to hang around down here.' Ghosts, he said, are of all shapes and sizes and to suit all tastes: benign, evil, violent, playful and sad.

A particularly sad ghost which the canon helped to free was that of a parson in his own diocese. The parson was a bachelor with homosexual tendencies and a feeling of inadequacy. His footsteps haunted the place after his death, and his presence hung so heavily in every room that his successor begged Canon Pearce-Higgins to exorcise the ghost.

The canon went to the vicarage accompanied by a medium, Miss Edna Taylor, and through her the sad ghost of the former parson spoke of the changes that had occurred since he died. He mentioned the names of several 'bad boys' at the youth club he had run, and otherwise established his identity. 'There was no doubt whatever as to who he was,' the canon asserted.

He told the sad ghost: 'You must go away.'

'I don't know where to go,' the ghost replied.

'You must go on into a higher realm of life,' ordered the determined canon.

Describing the case to me later, he said: 'The atmosphere of the vicarage had been dense and heavy, but after the exorcism service it lightened considerably – and the footsteps ceased.'

Then there was the case, described by Canon Pearce-Higgins as 'a perfectly ordinary case', which concerned an old man who had lived in a cottage at Kingston in Surrey. After his death the cottage had been pulled down and a new house had been built on the site. The old man's ghost did not like the change, it seemed, and wanted his old cottage back. The canon believed that he made contact with the ghost through a medium, explained the position regarding the cottage and said he would hold a service of exorcism to help the ghost on its way, which he did.

Canon Pearce-Higgins knew several cases of ghosts that had returned, seemingly deliberately, to haunt those who had done them an injustice during their earthly life.

One ghost which the canon 'soothed and persuaded to go away' was that of a man who had lived at Lewisham in London. For a long time the ghost terrified two brothers by stamping loudly up and down the stairs at dead of night. The canon discovered that the dead man had occupied a first-floor flat in the house for many years but when his wife died the brothers managed to force him out of the flat he had spent many happy years in, and moved him into the basement. 'After he died he evidently returned to show his disapproval!' Canon Pearce-Higgins told me. 'But I persuaded him that he had had his revenge and he could go away – and he went.'

I asked the canon once whether he had ever been frightened by a ghost, and he told me that during a lecture tour of America he had found himself awake in the middle of the night, when he was staying in an old farmhouse, and he was immediately aware of the presence of 'a supernatural being'. He saw nothing but he was really frightened. 'Oh it frightened me all right,' he told me. 'I prayed harder than I have ever done before; and in the morning I exorcized the place with bell, book and candle – and holy water too! That was a nasty one but I cleared it ...'

Another exorcism, not involving Canon Pearce-Higgins, that appears to have been succesful is recounted by Lynn Picknett in *Flights of Fancy?* and involves people 'well known' to the author. The case concerned a teenaged girl, 'Julie', the adopted daughter of a mentally disturbed woman, 'Mrs Hall', who was in her menopause. Lynn Picknett describes 'this explosive psychic mixture' as being exacerbated by the house they occupied, which had been built by 'Mr Hall's' father and seemed 'steeped' in 'resentments, family tensions and tragedies'.

Julie claimed to see the ghost of her grandfather on the upstairs landing, and visitors had been known to be affected by the atmosphere in the house, so that the family became isolated and were left to themselves.

Things built up to a climax when arguments developed, and contact between Julie and her mother became strained and difficult. Raps were heard in the vicinity of Julie's bed, usually around 3.30 in the early morning. One enormous and reverberating rap would awaken her, and as soon as she sat up, hoping it had been a dream that had awakened her, other loud raps would follow. Then her bedside lamp would switch itself on and off and 'scrabbling' sounds would be heard from the vicinity of the skirting-boards, yet it seems to have been quite definitely established that there were no mice or other vermin in the house.

The noises and disturbances would continue for perhaps half an hour, and then they would calm down and sometimes cease altogether. But soon, in the light of day, books would turn themselves upside down and fly about the house; once a book hit Julie on the back of the neck as she crossed the 'haunted' landing – and she was the only person in the house at the time: the book, when it hit her, did not seem to have any force behind it, and she was not hurt. Soon there were electrical malfunctions, with the television set especially seeming to be the centre of attention: the picture would become distorted and then right itself; the set would turn itself on and off; and sometimes the plug would jump out of its socket. Once, when jagged lines appeared on the screen, they were accompanied by the sound of a woman sobbing: this incident was witnessed by both Julie and her father.

At other times flames shot up from the back of the television set, and once these flames set the curtains alight. Julie quickly pulled down the curtains while her father unplugged the television set but then as abruptly as it had begun, the fire ceased and only the burned curtains remained to remind them of the frightening event. A few days later some of Julie's schoolbooks were discovered on fire, and a few weeks later a box of burnt-out candles was discovered in her wardrobe; the box itself was also charred but none of the clothes hanging nearby was even scorched. All the lightbulbs in the house blew out on the day before Julie's fifteenth birthday; the front door was discovered on fire, and neighbours said for weeks they had heard voices raised in anger and the sound of sobbing coming from the house.

Before long the Hall family moved out of the house, but the family who moved in experienced such a barrage of disturbances (raps and crashes, footfalls, flying crockery, moving objects and constant interference with the electrics in various rooms of the house) that they felt they were being attacked by something evil and decided to have the place exorcized.

The exorcism was conducted with considerable solemnity and involved the traditional bell, book and candle, thorough sprinkling of holy water, and prayers and incantations – and it seemed to work, although the new occupants moved out within a few months. They insisted, however, that it was not the disturbances that had caused them to move, and perhaps they were right, for later occupants of the house were, as far as can be established, completely untroubled by anything of a psychic nature.

Another London vicar who has carried out many exorcisms – he has reportedly claimed to have 'cast out 1,000 devils' – is the Rev. Christopher Neil-Smith, who has addressed members of the Ghost Club on the subject of exorcism. I remember he described one case where an 'evil spirit' had influenced a boy and landed him in a juvenile court for arson. Neil-Smith was apparently able to release the boy from the evil influence with his individual exorcism, which includes the firm physical handling of the afflicted person, on occasion.

Once, during the course of a television current affairs programme, Neil-Smith appeared with medium Eva Twigg and was shown exorcizing a 'wolf spirit' that was inhabiting the body of a young man, but in the main Neil-Smith works without a medium, because he told me he finds it confusing since, during the course of the exorcisms he carried out, he frequently gets 'direct communications'.

The Rev. Neil-Smith told Ghost Club members that he had seen his dead father clairvoyantly as a boy, in the Anglican church where his father had also served. 'He appeared to me and said I would enter the ministry, although I had no intention of doing so at the time.' This vicar is careful to make what he regards as a distinction between psychic and spiritual power. 'I would not use psychic forces,' he says, 'although maybe I am psychic myself; but the forces I use are essentially spiritual. I am not denying the psychic but this has to be controlled by spiritual powers.' For this reason he is against lay exorcists: 'The church may exorcize but when outsiders do it they are not controlled by spiritual forces.' The spiritualist press took him to task for this statement, I remember, and said: 'Nonsense vicar! We are all spirit beings; therefore we are all endowed with spiritual power and there is no evidence that God ordained anyone to speak or act for Him exclusively, whether in exorcism or in any other department of human affairs.'

Such exorcisms as those carried out by the Rev. Neil-Smith are aimed at Satan, and it has been suggested that a poltergeist is on a lower or less sinister level but nevertheless 'something evil from an evil place'. The history of poltergeists – those mischievous infestations that seem to be fond of adolescents – is full of attempts to exorcize the disturbances. Some of the early and well-attested poltergeist cases are no exception, and in the well-documented Wesley case (1716) the Rev. Samuel Wesley and others said prayers in attempts to exorcize 'Old Jeffrey', whose noisy activities have been meticulously recorded, and it has to be said that on occasion knocking sounds, described as 'a great noise', interrupted the Wesleys at prayer.

Another 'classic poltergeist case' is that of the *château* in Calvados, Normandy, described and recorded as 'the Château of T'. For well over ten years in the nineteenth century and, it seems, with hardly a pause for over three months at one period, the occupants were subjected to a wealth of 'diverse' and 'amazing' disturbances. A 'novena' (a devotion consisting of a prayer said on nine successive days, asking for some special blessing) was said at Lourdes for the peace of the castle and, we read, 'everything stopped'. For a while too all the disturbances ceased after the castle was exorcized, but then the trouble broke out again and, says Harry Price, '... continued intermittently for many years'.

Camille Flammarion (1842–1925), a president of the Society for Psychical Research, refers to the case in his volume *Haunted Houses*:

> After the exorcisms a great calm set in. One almost incredible thing took place which gave us much hope for the future ... medals of St Bénoît, indulgenced crosses, and Lourdes medals had been placed

on all the doors. These medals and crosses amounted to a good-sized package ... on the following morning a tremendous noise occurred and that next day medals and crosses had disappeared so that nothing could be found, though they and the doors were very numerous ... [Once] the exorcisms had ceased [they] were succeeded by several days of peace. You may imagine how agreeable these days were. But two or three days afterwards Madame was writing some lines on her knees by a little desk when suddenly an immense packet of medals and crosses fell in front of her on the desk ... They were all the medals placed on the doors except those of Lourdes.

The good priest of T –. who, like myself, knew the sincerity and honesty of the castle people and wished to keep them in his parish, said to them: 'Have courage; the Devil surrenders his arms; everything is finished I can assure you. You will now be left in peace.' But privately the good man said: 'I am still much afraid, because the Lourdes medals have not come back.'

And come back the disturbances assuredly did, with loud and quick knocks and 'a great noise in the drawing-room'; heavy objects were moved and furniture was arranged in a semi-circle: this happened inside a locked room. The sound of music was heard emanating from the corner of another room; bolts were drawn and candles blown out; heavy crashing noises were repeatedly heard and organ music sounded from the *château* when there were no human beings inside ...

This professional astronomer of the first rank and an eminent psychical researcher, author of scientific works and an associate of Alfred Russell Wallace (who formulated the theory of evolution almost simultaneously with Charles Darwin), ends his report on the case by saying, 'It is one of the best-established cases within our knowledge ... it seems to me that we cannot but feel authorised to conclude from all this that *there are invisible beings.*'

The seventeenth-century Drummer of Tedworth case, investigated by the Rev. Joseph Glanvill, chaplain to Charles II and a Fellow of the Royal Society, affected the house of John Mompesson, a prominent Wiltshire magistrate, for some twelve months. The drumming sounds, heard and verified by many people of standing, seemed to '... withdraw into the cock-loft during prayer time but returned as soon as prayers were done'. As is the case with most poltergeists (and Harry Price referred to this case as 'a classic – if not *the* classic – amongst poltergeist cases'), exorcism did not seem to be completely effective.

In the case of the Ringcroft Poltergeist (1695), incidents included unexplained fires, the setting loose of cattle, stones thrown all over the house over a period of *several days*, the movement of objects, unexplained knocks and bangings, and some members of the family were reportedly beaten with staves and driven out of the house ...

During one attempt at exorcism by prayers at Ringcroft, some small stones were thrown at the parson praying, and yet it was noticed that for a time no stones were thrown on a Sunday. Another time a disembodied voice cried, 'Hush, Hush,' at the close of every sentence of the exorcism, and the family dog, hearing the unfamiliar voice, would run to the door and bark. At other times during prayers '... the entity would whistle and groan and sometimes lumps of burning peat were thrown in the direction of those at prayer.

Once five ministers attempted to exorcize the ghost, but stones were thrown so violently and so frequently at them and throughout the house that the whole property seemed to shake. A hole appeared in the room, and through it a great many more stones fell into the house. One clergyman was hit on the back but, in the nature of the poltergeist-projected objects, '... he suffered no hurt.' The point is that five clergymen attested to the phenomena, and their combined attempts at exorcism failed. Four weeks later the disturbances ceased as abruptly and as mysteriously as they had commenced.

Some 250 years later, in 1943, a poltergeist infestation occurred at a house near Poitiers, France, when not only were objects moved and in some cases raised to the ceiling and remained there, suspended in mid-air, but a 16-year-old girl, Geneviève, was lifted 'by supernatural agency' and thrown to the foot of her bed! When she and her mother were seated in another room, their chairs '... were whisked away from under them and then overturned'. The girl then left the house and a priest was called in. He exorcized the place and 'all was quiet'.

Geneviève, thinking all was well, returned to the house – and an oaken dresser moved by itself from the wall and crashed to the floor, and a table '... nearly crushed a policeman – according to his sworn statement'. Then the mantle top of a table was cracked by a violent but unseen blow; and, as Harry Price puts it, '... since neither prayer nor police could stop the trouble, all the occupants moved out of the house'.

At ghost-ridden Ballechin House in 1892, reputedly haunted for some twenty years, a Jesuit priest, Father Hayden, detailed in writing his personal experiences in the house for John, third Marquess of Bute, who was deeply interested in psychic matters.

After hearing loud noises between his bed and the ceiling, 'like continuous explosions of small bombs', so loud he could not hear himself speak, he changed his room, but the noises followed him. He also heard raps, shrieks, screams and the sound 'like that of a large animal thrusting itself against the outside of the bedroom door', and he decided to attempt an exorcism.

He sprinkled all the rooms in the house with holy water and recited the *Visita quaesumus*, a prayer for the divine protection of a house and its occupants, in every part of the house, but all to no purpose. Later a Catholic archbishop tried to exorcize the ghost but with no better results.

At Borley, known as 'the most haunted house in England' before Harry Price had even heard of the place, several efforts at exorcism were conducted. The story of the Borley haunting has been told in no fewer than four full-length books, a dozen radio and television programmes, scores of scientific reports and innumerable newspaper and magazine articles. In brief, Borley Rectory in Essex was built in 1863 by the Rev. H.D.E. Bull and immediately occupied by him and his large family; he was succeeded by his son, the Rev. 'Harry' Bull, in 1892, who was followed by the Rev. G. Eric Smith in 1928, by the Rev. Lionel A. Foyster in 1930 and by the Rev. A.C. Henning (who never lived in the haunted rectory) in 1936. It must surely be significant that *everyone* who lived at the rectory from 1863 until 1939, when the building was destroyed by fire – four successive rectors, their wives and families, all asserted they heard, saw and felt things they could not explain. In particular the ghost of a nun was seen in the garden, and especially on a particular grass path in the garden so often that the path became known as 'the Nun's Walk'.

At Borley Rectory reported phenomena over a long period included materializations of the nun and also an unidentified man and a girl in blue; horses and a coach; audible phenomena, including a woman's voice, whisperings, the sound of galloping hooves, padding sounds, music, bell-ringing, footsteps, raps, taps and knockings; these were displaced or projected objects; door-locking and unlocking; while visual phenomena also included wall- and paper-writing; lights in windows of empty rooms, keys falling from locks, window blinds swinging, fires and smoke; miscellaneous phenomena included odours (pleasant and unpleasant), coldness, touchings, unidentified footsteps in snow, a gluey substance, face-slapping, reaction by animals and affected apparatus. These and other activities were reported by upwards of *eighty* witnesses.

In the long history of strange happenings at Borley, it is understandable that attempts should have been made at exorcism. One day in June 1931, when 'messages' appealing for 'light', 'Mass', 'prayers' and 'help' were appearing mysteriously on the walls of the rectory, Dom Richard Whitehouse was present (as he told me himself), and several times he and the rector and the rector's wife, Marianne Foyster, knelt down and addressed the Holy Trinity, asking where, if the messages were genuine, the Mass should be offered. A few moments later, on again passing the spot where they had knelt and asked this question, they found the word 'here' had been written on the wall.

The late Guy P.J. L'Estrange, a justice of the peace and a local figure of some standing, told me of experiencing a wealth of paranormal activity at Borley Rectory in 1932. Soon after he arrived on a visit, there was a loud ringing of bells from downstairs. The rector (Lionel Foyster) and his wife took L'Estrange to the bannister and showed him the bells in the kitchen passage below all clanging wildly although, because of the trouble and disturbance with this bell-ringing, at this time all the bell-wires had been cut. Yet the bell-ringing continued, and Guy L'Estrange tried to communicate with the unseen entities responsible.

'If some invisible person is person is present and can hear my words,' he cried, looking up at the bells, high overhead (they had now gone down into the kitchen passage), 'please stop these bells ringing.' Instantly every bell became silent. 'And I do mean instantly,' L'Estrange told me. 'I do not mean that they gradually slowed down, as one would expect. No, it was as though each had been seized and held by a hidden hand.'

After a lot of bell-ringing and other disturbances, the rector decided to seek relief in prayer, as he details in his unpublished manuscript, 'Fifteen Months in a Haunted House', and he, his wife and L'Estrange and his companions adjourned to the chapel on the first floor over the front door, taking with them a relic of the Curé d'Ars (Jean-Baptiste Vianney, 1786-1859). They then proceeded from room to room, making the sign of the cross with the relic, and for a while the incessant noises ceased.

Later, in his bedroom, still accompanied by his friends, Guy L'Estrange noticed that the air '... seemed to get much colder within a few minutes', and everyone present saw a patch of luminosity become larger and denser until it resembled the shape of a human being in robes. Guy L'Estrange addressed the figure but there was no reply. He approached it and had the impression that he was pushed back. He resisted and came to a standstill. 'Won't you let me help you?' he asked. There was no reply, and after a few seconds the apparition faded.

Before he left Borley Rectory, L'Estrange told the rector and his wife that he had a strong feeling that his exorcisms – he had apparently tried several different ones – had been successful and that there would be no more disturbances, but, he told me, it was obvious they did not share his confidence. Only a week later, however, he received a letter from Lionel Foyster in which he declared that no more trouble had in fact been experienced in the house and that there was 'quite a different feeling throughout the whole building'. 'I only trust,' he added, 'that this will continue'. Apparently it did too, for three years later the rector wrote to L'Estrange saying, 'This house is now practically normal'.

Earlier, in March 1931, it is interesting to recall, the Rev. Lionel Foyster had invited two Anglican priests to see what they could do. One of them was the Rev. Clive Luget, who himself told me of this visit. He and his brother clergyman went over the house with incense and holy water obtained especially from the well of Our Lady of Walsingham, attempting a mild form of exorcism, and when this had no effects, they performed an elaborate exorcism rite, followed by complete fumigation of the house with creosote. They also enlisted the help of two clergymen friends, and the four priests sprinkled holy water, blessed the house from top to bottom and prayed and exorcized every room; but all this had little lasting effect.

The Rev. A.C. Henning, rector of Borley from 1936 to 1955, had many curious experiences at Borley, both in the rectory, before it was destroyed by fire in 1939, and in the church and churchyard just across the road. Indeed he compiled a booklet entitled *Haunted Borley*, and he carried out several services of exorcism on the site, in the cottage adjoining the site, and in and around the church; and he buried the fragmentary human remains, which he believed were those of the ghost nun, that had been unearthed on the rectory site, in Liston churchyard – an act he regarded, as he told me, as exorcism *par excellence*! He was frequently asked to hold a Requiem Mass for the ghost nun and, although he held it to be a grievous omission to neglect prayers for the departed, he did not feel he could hold such a service for a being whose identity was so shadowy, and so he held no specific Mass for the ghost nun, but he took part in several attempts at exorcism at Borley; this quiet-spoken, gentle and kindly priest trying in the best way he knew to lay the ghost to rest.

Interestingly enough, on All Souls' Day 1947 the Rev. A.C. Henning did pray for an unquiet spirit at a Requiem Mass conducted in Borley churchyard, and for a while, he told me, things did seem to quieten down.

Once, in 1937, when Sir George and Lady Whitehouse, neighbours and friends of the Foysters (Dom Richard Whitehouse was the nephew of Lady Whitehouse), were visiting Borley Rectory, they experienced a wealth of extraordinary happenings which included movement of objects, bell-ringing, written messages all over the house on scraps of paper, outbreaks of fire, and the sudden appearance of a stone, the size of a hen's egg, and then two more stones that came from the empty upper regions of the house, one hitting the rector's wife on the shoulder. Lady Whitehouse went home to Arthur Hall and returned with some dried lavender, as she had found that incense and sweet odours sometimes quietened things. Some of the lavender was scattered onto glowing embers, then scooped up on a shovel, and this was taken through the house in an attempt at fumigation. While they were passing through the Foysters' bedroom, a shower of small stones fell around Lady Whitehouse and Mrs Foyster, who carried out this singular exorcism. It had no effect, however, and in fact things became so bad that, as midnight approached, the Foysters and two sleepy children (adopted by the Foysters) were taken to the Whitehouse home, where they all stayed for several days.

With the disappearance of the haunted rectory, first by fire and then by demolition, the site itself was reportedly haunted, and there are literally hundreds of reports of apparently inexplicable happenings encountered by different people on different occasions. One man who felt that an exorcism of the rectory site might help matters was John May of Bury St Edmunds. He visited the site in July 1946, and I cannot do better than quote from the letter he sent to me afterwards, detailing his exorcism.

I have been very successful in exorcizing unquiet spirits and I have been familiar with the tales of the Borley Rectory hauntings for many years. On a hot July day in 1946 I decided to cycle over to Borley from Redgrave. I would stress the fact that it was a very hot sultry day with more than a hint of thundery storm in the air; the sky was clear, blue and cloudless. I reached the old Rectory gate about two o'clock when the heat of the afternoon was at its greatest. I recall that I was perspiring as I leaned my bicycle against the hedge. I stood in the shade of the tree where the nun is said to have materialized, in order to cool off a little, and noticed nothing strange; it was a typical forlorn and unkept garden. I moved over to the right from the shade to where the sun was flecking the ground through the leaves of tall bushes. The ground was littered with dead leaves and the dead branches of the bushes. Without warning, and very suddenly, I sensed a cold wave of air. It was not the coolness of a breeze – but the sticky, damp, raw cold, that one would expect to meet on entering a deep underground tomb. So great was my awareness of this cold that I started back to my bicycle to get my jacket. It was then that the most extraordinary phenomenon of the afternoon began. A stout stick rose seemingly unaided from the ground and waved itself about six inches from my nose. It waved backwards and forwards for several inches, then soared away in a arc and fell some distance away among the shrubs.

I thereupon said a prayer, taken from an old manuscript of exorcism which I came upon in Rome during the War: 'Oh unquiet spirit, who at thy release from the contagion of the flesh choosest to remain earthbound and haunt this spot, go thy way, rejoicing that the prayers of the faithful shall follow thee, that thou mayest enjoy everlasting rest and peace, and at the end mayest find thy rightful place at the Throne of Grace, Amen.'

Alas, whoever or whatever was active on the site of the burnt-out rectory did not respond to Mr May's prayer, and unexplained incidents continued to be reported. In fact, as Harry Price stated in his *End of Borley Rectory*, 'Exorcisms by

Anglican and Roman Catholic priests and by lay exorcists failed to stop the phenomena.'

Some forty years ago I spent several years investigating the fascinating haunting of Langenhoe church on the Essex marshes. It was a unique case in many ways, with apparitions, doors slamming and locking by themselves, footsteps (both inside and outside the church), movement of objects (both inside and outside the church), odours (pleasant and unpleasant) and 'monkish' music and chanting and bell-ringing. I detail much of this remarkable case of haunting in my volume *A Host of Hauntings*, but I did not mention the exorcisms that the rector and others carried out there.

The Rev. Ernest Merryweather was in his sixties when I knew him; a large, easy-going and kindly man who had never experienced any kind of paranormal activity in many years ministry – until he came to Langenhoe. Once, when he was attempting a blessing, a small sanctuary lamp on the altar of St George burst into flames, and the rector had to rush down the church with a dust-cover to extinguish the flames. Another time, when he was performing a similar service, he sensed someone was behind him, although he knew he was quite alone in the church. He turned round and saw a female figure that he took to be a novice move from behind a memorial to the south wall of the tower where the wall seemed to open, and she passed in; then the wall closed up again. Strangely enough, a completely independent witness claimed to have seen a very similar figure outside the church, and she disappeared into the wall of the church; if she had passed through the wall and continued inside the church, she would have been in the position in which the rector saw her! Both witnesses, who were unaware of the other's testimony, described the figure as wearing a veil over her head and shoulders and walking with a slight stoop.

On another occasion when Mr Merryweather was attempting to carry out a 'special blessing', a form of exorcism in fact, some of the hanging lamps began to swing backwards and forwards; and on yet another, similar occasion a month later, when he opened his eyes, one of the candles on the altar of St George had completely disappeared!

Three months later, during yet another 'blessing', the rector and four companions were startled by a loud bang, and they discovered that one of the lamp glasses had exploded. Finally, during the course of a full service of exorcism when Mr Merryweather was assisted by three fellow clergymen, 'the priest's door' opened by itself and then closed, and all four priests heard footsteps that seemed to progress from the priest's door to the vestry door, which remained closed, but the footsteps seemed to pass through the door and then there was silence. The clergymen resumed their exorcism but, as Mr Merryweather was in the habit of saying, 'Nothing seems to placate the ghosts of Langenhoe.' Before long, however, he retired from the ministry, the living of Langenhoe was combined with that of a neighbouring parish and after standing empty and alone with its ghosts for a few years the church fell into decay and was finally pulled down. Today nothing marks the site of what could well have been the most haunted church in England.

8 More Exorcisms in Haunted Houses, etc.

Sir Shane Leslie may have believed, apropos exorcism: 'If there is a ghost or a wandering soul in a haunted house, the saying of prayers or Masses is the proper course; in the case of obsession or diabolical intervention the Church has provided Exorcism; prayers and holy water have a soothing effect in the one case but rather tumultuous resistance in the case of the other ...' I say, would that it were so simple!

An amusing and completely understandable reaction to an uneventful night in a haunted house is recorded by Father Cyril Martindale[1] in a letter to Sir Shane. He writes: 'There had been several attempts at suicide on the premises and an alleged Sense of Evil in one particular room which (also allegedly) much alarmed a hefty Rugger player ... I was asked to go and stay there, so I did, not feeling at all the right person for such enterprises. I sat up in the room, with a breviary, patience cards, my rosary round my neck, a thriller, and positively steaming with Holy Water. The Horror was alleged to horr at 2.00 a.m. I stayed there until after 3.00 in an even worse temper and nothing whatsoever happened to me then or later. Next day I blessed the various rooms, calling such spirits as might be about by the most insulting names and then apologizing in case they might be quite nice ones and the Evil (if any) in the people they met and not in them ...'

It was Sir Shane Leslie who told me about a poltergeist infestation in 1914 that was investigated and exorcized by no fewer than three priests. After Cardinal Moran attempted, unsuccessfully, to deal with the trouble, Bishop McKenna of Clogher visited the afflicted house and, deciding that the entity was diabolical, authorized Dean Keown to exorcize it but, having no more success than the cardinal, he withdrew and suggested that the hand of the bishop might be more effective.

The case centred around two innocent girls, touching puberty, who were bewildered by what was happening around them, which culminated in 'mischievous forms of spirit life' manifesting themselves. The origin of the ghostly manifestations was thought to date from the murder in the house of an old-age pensioner, on the day he had drawn his pension. In Sir Shane's opinion this may have '... opened the way for the poltergeist', but the only ghost described by witnesses was very unlike an elderly pensioner. One man said he saw a ghostly form that looked like 'a ball of wool in a black bag'.

The house, possibly on account of the reportedly inexplicable happenings, passed through several hands fairly quickly, one family occupying it for only *one* night, but they kept very quiet about what they had experienced and sold the house soon afterwards. The two daughters of the next family who purchased the house found their pillows repeatedly 'torn from under their heads'. A priest who visited the house told Sir Shane that he had *heard* the ghost 'snoring in the dark', and when he sat on the vacant bed, it felt as if snakes were moving under him. When he switched on the light, he saw what appeared to be a human bulk under the sheets, a form that promptly collapsed – and then a new swelling developed in the bed, and again the priest heard the snoring sound. When the priest used holy water, the entity showed 'Protestant hostility' and seemed infuriated; when the priest placed the sacred pyx – the vessel in which the Host is preserved – on the bed, there was considerable disturbance and a loud noise which seemed to sink into the floor and deeper still into the earth below, but still the sound 'echoed from the depths'.

This particular priest visited the house more than fifty times, and he testified that the presence of the ghost usually manifested at first, 'like the sound of straw in the air'; it seemed to be fascinated by the bedstead occupied by the young girls, and time after time the bedcovers were interfered with when no human person was anywhere near. Once he saw a human form raise itself under the sheets of the empty bed, then the form collapsed and there was movement under the sheet that suggested to the priest the idea that an animal of some kind was there; on occasion the priest felt considerable fear, especially when 'something' seemed to spit at him!

Once, when the mother and the two girls were sleeping on pallets around a fire in the living-room to get away from the haunted room, everyone heard a sound like that of a kicking horse, and the bedclothes were thrown across the room. Another time, when the two girls were in bed, the priest held them by their four hands in one of his hands and laid his other hand over their feet. The phenomena (movement under the bedclothes and noises from the bedstead) continued, and he was convinced that the girls could not have been responsible.

Another night, when he voiced the opinion that whatever was there came from Hell, there was a loud hissing sound. Taking his courage in both hands, he stood beside the empty bed and challenged the ghost. He clearly felt someone or some thing moving under the bedclothes – something alive; then he had the feeling of something resembling an eel twisting round his wrist, but it went no further and he realized that it did not dare touch his consecrated hand. He remained in the same position for what seemed a very long time, and at length the movements in the bed ceased.

A canon told Sir Shane Leslie that he visited the house at least sixteen times, and once he heard a musical, whistling sound that seemed to come from the ceiling. He used holy water copiously, and this appeared to vex whatever was in the room, and it moved further and further along the wall away from the water, making loud knocking sounds as it went. When a full Mass was said in the kitchen, there was some relief, and the family at last obtained some rest.

Another time, as the girls sat on a stool side by side, a cracking sound worked its way round them. When the priest cracked his thumb, the 'presence' cracked louder still. He asked for nine raps to represent 'yes' and they came. He tried Irish and Latin and received sensible answers every time. He asked how many of his family were born in County Monaghan – which no one knew except him – and the answer was correct. The pet dog of the family was in another room, and the priest asked, 'Could you put the dog from under the bed?' and immediately the collie came out from under the bed, 'dancing mad, with blazing, fear-crazed eyes'.

Eventually (there were many more well-attested but seemingly quite inexplicable happenings) during a particularly noisy period two visiting priests asked the girls' mother to get

into the 'haunted' bed. She did so, and when there was no
movement, they then asked each of the girls to do the same in
turn, with the same result. All the time, however, there were
sounds in the room of 'comings and goings, loud and distinct'
that were certainly not made by any of those present.

Finally one of the priests had the Blessed Sacrament with him
and, lowering the light, he took out the pyx and made the sign
of the cross over it, over the bed, unknown to the mother and
the two girls. This had no sooner been done than the noise
increased a hundredfold. 'All the noises imaginable were made,
before the evil spirit suddenly disappeared and did not
reappear.'

The Rev. Trevor Dearing, a former vicar of Hainault in Essex,
became well known for seeming miracles of healing that took
place through his ministry, but more particularly for his
'ministry of exorcism' which he has, incidentally, continued
during his work in Northamptonshire. In Essex he held weekly
services at which apparent exorcisms were by no means
uncommon. During one televized service a deep voice
emanated from the body of a young prostitute: 'No, no, I won't
go out of her ...' Already the psychiatrists had given up on the
girl, but Trevor Dearing believed he could help. He laid his
hands on her shoulders and attempted to take authority over
the spirit possessing the girl.

'No, no, don't cast me out ...' screamed the harsh voice from
the usually quiet-voiced girl.

'Jesus is alive,' repeated the priest. 'Go, mocking spirit ...'

The girl slumped to the floor, screaming, and Trevor Dearing
turned to the congregation. 'Can we all pray?' he asked, 'I am
going to minister to her. Everyone sing quietly, "Jesus Breaks
Every Fetter".'

As the hymn was sung, the vicar laid his hands firmly on the
girl. Shaking his head with determination, he announced: 'I
come now to cast you out ...' The sound of singing and that of
people praying grew louder, and in an air of expectancy the
clergyman continued: 'I command you, in the name of Jesus! I
forbid you to speak blasphemy. You *shall* go out of the body of
this woman. You shall *not* hurt this girl or anyone else any more.
Go, in the name of Jesus. Go now ...' Then he shouted the word
'Out!' and immediately the girl became relaxed, silent and

seemingly at peace. She looked flushed and seemed dazed and unaware of all that had taken place – weakened, without doubt, but certainly peaceful and troubled no more by the 'something' that had been possessing her. Later she said she felt the exorcism had changed her life.

Trevor Dearing once told me that he had exorcized – or 'delivered', as he prefers to call it, since clergymen are still forbidden to perform exorcisms without the blessing of their bishop – no fewer than a thousand demons in four years. He tells his story in a volume entitled *Exit the Devil*, and I am sure he is very sincere in his approach to the subject and in his desire to help. I have to say that I remain to be convinced that the 'devils' he claims to cast out are always independent entities, but I am quite sure that he has done much valuable work in a very difficult field.

As recently as June 1988, Trevor Dearing visited a haunted council house in Peterborough. Here the 'terrified' Pluck family left their home claiming they had experienced the smell of burning flesh in one of the bedrooms; they had heard a child's voice call 'Daddy'; dogs had repeatedly refused to enter the house; there was frequently a feeling of intense coldness on the upper stairway; a 'mist-like vapour' was seen to pass through the body of one member of the family, and the figure of a child had been seen in the house.

Local council officials turned to the Church for help and reported afterwards that, '... thorough investigation, including some by the Church, had uncovered no evidence of the supernatural.' The housing manager, Trevor Redshaw, added, 'The tenants became very concerned and absolutely terrified of living in the house because of what they felt were manifestations of the supernatural. The church investigated but could not confirm that this was so. The Council checked all the main services and could not find anything physically wrong.'

Trevor Dearing is quoted as saying that what the family claimed was, in his experience, very credible. I understand that an exorcism of sorts was carried out at the house, where, according to neighbours, everything was fine until the Pluck family started to dig up the drive. It often happens that alterations or interference with existing buildings or areas *does* seem to promote psychic phenomena, so perhaps this is an area that could have been explored. In the event the Pluck family were given a new council house, and their last words on the matter were: 'We just want to forget about it.'

Another council house where services of exorcism did seem to have some effect was situated in Winteringham Road, Grimsby. For several months in 1981 the Currier family experienced a wealth of strange happenings; things went from bad to worse, and night after night the young parents and their two small children found themselves 'terrified' by ghostly appearances and unexplained happenings. Things became so bad that the family, fled from the house and moved in with friends nearby.

John and Pat Currier recalled hearing stories of exorcism with bell, book and candle, and they contacted Canon Geoffrey Brown, who visited the house and conducted a service of prayer in every room. Afterwards he told a Ghost Club investigator that he was quietly confident that 'the combined forces of good' would banish any evil forces from the house.

In the event, things did not improve sufficiently for the Currier family to move back, and a further, more powerful and more impressive 'exorcism' was planned. Meanwhile two Ghost Club investigators spent a night at the house and reported several curious incidents. The family said things were still very bad.

The young couple, John Currier, a fisherman, and his wife, Pat, said they regularly saw the figure of a man, a woman and a child standing beside the bed of their eighteen-month-old son, Paul. They also asserted that chairs had crossed the room without anyone's touching them, in front of several witnesses; doors had opened and closed of their own accord; curtains in the 'haunted bedroom' moved backwards and forwards as they watched …

Several times they were awakened in the middle of the night by Paul's screaming, and when they went to him he said three people were leaning over him. The Ghost Club investigators discovered that neighbours too had seen ghostly figures in the house, and when Canon Geoffrey Brown heard all this, he agreed to a further visit and additional prayers.

Accompanied by three parish priests and by the occupants of the house and friends of the family, Canon Brown again blessed each room in the house, the children holding candles, the clergymen crucifixes and Bibles as they passed from room to room. Everyone joined in the services of prayers, and Canon

Brown emphasized afterwards that he had not actually conducted a service of exorcism (although that is what it amounted to), rather he called it a service of prayer such as might be held for anyone who was sick or badly needed help. 'We merely asked God to make the Curriers' house a place where good can triumph over evil,' he added.

Later a medium was called to the house but she had no more success than the Church, and then, seemingly of their own accord, the disturbances became less frequent, less distinct and less troublesome and before long the house was no longer affected by anything frightening – possibly the 'exorcism' did have an effect, but a delayed one.

I discuss another ecclesiastical haunting in my autobiography, *No Common Task*. It came to my notice that a vicar was closing his Berkshire church because of 'the presence of dark forces'. I wrote to him and he invited me down for a chat, having told me in his reply that the church in question was closed for financial reasons, but odd things did take place shortly after he was inducted to the parish some years before. After he had talked to his bishop, a spiritualist medium visited the place and 'cleansed' the church and vicarage. This man said the spirits of a number of virgins had remained on the site after they had been sacrificed many, many years ago. Subsequently another vicar who specialized in exorcisms came down several times, and he too had carried out services of exorcism, but still the place was 'undoubtedly haunted'. For a number of reasons I do not propose to identify the vicar or the parish, but the verbatim records are available and the case was again in the news in 1989 when there were plans to demolish the 'haunted' church.

The original report that I saw quoted the vicar as saying: 'There is much that I would like to say about the evil here,' and his wife is quoted as saying: 'We have not imagined any of this. There is evil here. It has driven people from the church. It is real and it is frightening. Nine years ago the then bishop called for an exorcism after windows had been broken, vestments taken and candles unaccountably lit. The exorcist found a subtle force, certainly evil, and believed that the church had probably been built on a pagan burial-ground. It is not mere vandalism, it is more than that; I have felt physical pain. I have been frightened and it may sound irrational but there are forces here to be reckoned with. After the last exorcism these forces seemed less

strong but they are still here. The congregation used to be large
in this fine family church; once we had a thousand people here.
The church is to be closed and the devil has won this time but it
is not the end of the story. The evil here will be driven out.'

The vicar who carried out that latter exorcism was quoted as
saying: 'There certainly was an evil presence there when I did
the cleansing ceremony. It was one of the most unpleasant I've
ever done. There were some very disturbed spirits there.'

My wife and I went to see the vicar and his wife and found
them a charming couple, very willing to discuss the difficulties
they had experienced, in an open and sensible way, always
looking first for a rational explanation before considering any
other possibility. They told us that the vicarage was in fact more
haunted than the church, and we were welcome to come down
and hear the full story and carry out an investigation. We spent
some time in the nearby church, and there was a very curious
atmosphere there, even then; an expectant, waiting feeling that
was very apparent. Both my wife and I felt this atmosphere
immediately on entering the church; a feeling neither of us had
ever experienced in a church before, nor have we since, 'An aura
of evil' would be an apt description.

Armed with their apparatus, eight members of the Ghost Club
descended on the vicarage and church and spent an interesting
night hearing about the disturbances and carrying out various
investigations and experiments, especially at the vicarage. The
unexplained happenings, we were told, included the deliberate
tripping up of the vicar's wife and one of their children,
resulting in some badly cut legs; the sounds of footsteps and the
rattling of a heavy letter-box on the front door, followed by the
sound of running footsteps. This happened many times, but
there was never any letter or message or any physical
explanation for the sound of footsteps.

Much later the vicar learned that the first incumbent had been
a typical Victorian tyrant of a father; he had five daughters and
was very strict with them, never allowing any of them to have
gentlemen callers or in any way to associate with young men.
However, some of them were very persistent, as young men
tend to be, and at quiet moments they would write a note to the
girl concerned and slip it through the letter-box and hurriedly
run off. The girls' father – who habitually used the front room of
the house as an office, situated just inside the front door –

always heard the letter-box rattle, and he would be out of his room and intercept any message before the girls could reach it. It occurred to us that something of the tension and frustration and anger associated with this often-repeated incident may somehow have become locked into the atmosphere, to be repeated, in sound, many years later.

One exorcist who had visited and explored the house maintained that there were three bedrooms where the spirits of three girls were individually impressed, and he said he had 'released the chained souls'. We were told that each of the present incumbent's children had seen unexplained figures over the years, in the bedrooms indicated and also on a turning of one of the stairways. There had also been instances of apparent possession, when the vicar himself seemed to be 'taken over' by some malevolent influence and acted completely out of character. Once his wife awoke to hear her husband speaking in a strange voice, and once she was nearly strangled by an invisible entity. The list of possibly subjective but very frightening happenings was a lengthy and varied one.

All the occupants had come to feel that the front room of the house was the most haunted part, and they frequently felt that it had 'a terrible atmosphere'. It was decided that attempts would be made to contact any entity which might be present in the house, and séances were held in the 'haunted room'. We carefully removed an antique circular table with 'birdcage' fitment into the front room, and everyone present, including the vicar and his wife, took part in dimmed light in the first attempted séance. There was no response, and after some time the séance was abandoned and the vicar retired to bed.

Later, hoping to achieve some result, four members of the visiting party sat again, one of them a sensitive and experienced investigator, using the same table. Once again nothing happened. Requests were made for some raps or tilting of the table to indicate the possible presence of an invisible entity. The participants were changed and a glass and letters tried, but all to no avail, although the glass did show some signs of movement at one stage. After a rest we tried yet again, our sensitive member saying she felt sure some entity was present, and encouraging 'it' to manifest. Eventually a few raps sounded, and then there was silence. We rested and then once more: this time there did seem to be some force trying to move not only the glass but the table itself, and, as before, we verbally requested some sign of a presence, either by table-tilting or turning. After a few moments the table seemed to shudder, and we all expected it to tilt, but instead the top slid round to the right and we now discovered something none of us had previously known, and which is not normal for that kind of table: the top revolved on the base. It now proceeded to move under the hands of the sitters.

One lady member quickly established a code whereby movement of the table to the right meant 'yes' and movement to the left meant 'no', and by this means the sitters obtained answers to leading questions that suggested that the communicating entity was responsible for the death of someone in the house, a child whose body had been buried in the garden, beside a bush. The communicating entity appeared to be unhappy, and requested prayer. The Lord's Prayer was recited, and at the end the table became still and did not move again.

Later, when we began to relate something of what had happened to the rest of the party, who were in the next room, the vicar's wife interjected to say she always thought there was something very odd about one part of the garden, near a bush; she always had a feeling of sadness there, and to everyone's astonishment she said she had often wondered whether a child could have been buried there.

After our visit we were able to write to the vicar saying that we thought the atmosphere of the 'haunted room' was much better and that the whole house was now probably clear of any malevolent influence. We asked to be advised of any subsequent disturbances of any kind, and since we heard nothing we assume that all was well after our visit.

The brilliant character-actor C. Aubrey Smith (1863–1948) had a daughter, Mrs Honor Cobb, who tells me that she had many 'odd happenings' with her father who was the undisputed king of Hollywood's cricket-loving British colony (he introduced the game to Hollywood); he was a great personal friend of Boris Karloff, another cricket fanatic, and they once represented the film capital against a touring Australian team that included Bradman and McCabe; incidentally, Aubrey Smith was always a very sensitive water-diviner.

On one occasion, his daughter told me, in her eighty-seventh

year, he took part in a table-turning session with some friends
and found himself to be the last one with his hands on the table
that seemed positively alive! He had joined the party in a jovial
and not-too-serious mood, but the table soon began to move and
then really to whirl round and rock with definite motion – with
no one pushing it – and in the end Aubrey found the table
literally moving against him and he ended up pinned into a
corner of the room. As he always said when relating the
incident, he then realized that it was no laughing matter!

He and his wife once looked over a house in Britain when
they were going to be there for some months, but while his wife
loved the place, which did seem utterly charming, Aubrey
would not think of having it on any account. He had
encountered 'something' in the garden, and he took his little
daughter there without saying anything and she too said she felt
an 'invisible presence' at the same spot. Aubrey Smith thought
there had been a bad haunting associated with the house, and
he also felt that several exorcisms had taken place there:
exorcisms that had been only partially successful for something
was still left behind that could be detected by sensitive people. If
such a property was lived in by people who were aware of such
things and alive to the possibility of such happenings, Aubrey
felt that 'things might easily start up again'. Curiously enough, it
subsequently transpired that the house had indeed been badly
haunted at one time; there had been more than one murder in
either the house or garden; and a series of exorcisms had almost
cleared the place. The house, they learned, was 'very much
better' but 'something still lingered' in the garden.

In 1941 the actor Conrad Veidt (1893–1943) was living in
London, and I went to see him, mainly because I admired his
work on the stage and in the cinema but also because I had
heard the house he was living in was haunted. In common with
Boris Karloff and some other actors who specialized in sinister
roles, Veidt was a charming man in private life, full of old-world
courtesy, and he made time to tell me about the haunting and
about the exorcism he had taken part in. Years later Dr Paul
Tabori, who had himself worked with Alexander Korda, for
whom Conrad Veidt had made *The Spy in Black*, *Dark Journey* and
The Thief of Baghdad, told me all about Conrad Veidt's great
interest in occult matters, about the haunted house he had once
lived in and the exorcism he never tired of talking about.

The Veidts found the house in North London to be haunted very soon after they moved in. They were subjected to sounds of voices raised in argument; sudden bangs and crashing sounds at all times of the day and night; and the occasional appearance of visual phantom forms, sometimes a man, usually at the top of the stairway, sometimes a woman, usually on the stairway, and sometimes the pair together, glimpsed in one of the back bedrooms.

Conrad Veidt, interested and sympathetic as he was, found the disturbances interfering with his work and concentration and study of the demanding roles he had in hand and when he mentioned the matter to a friend, the possibility of exorcism was suggested. Meanwhile a friend of Lily and Conrad Veidt, being aware of the situation, independently discussed the matter with a clergyman friend who also suggested some sort of exorcism as the probable answer. So it came about that a service that amounted to an exorcism was carried out at the house.

Conrad Veidt himself viewed the proceedings with some scepticism but considerable interest, and on the appointed night he was present throughout the ceremony. He said afterwards that he had been most impressed by the pomp, solemnity and sincerity of the event, which began with two clergymen each blessing the house with prayers and words of benediction. They visited every part of the house and performed a complete ritual in each room. They also sprinkled holy water, left Bibles open throughout the house and rang credence bells as they left each room.

All was quiet, and the atmosphere throughout the house seemed to improve as they progressed – and then they arrived at the 'haunted' back bedroom. As the party entered that deserted and cold room, all those present saw, momentarily, the ghostly forms of the man and the woman that haunted the house. They were standing together in one corner of the room in a defiant and almost threatening attitude. The two clergymen hesitated for a moment but then walked straight at the figures, and as they drew near, the forms dissolved and disappeared. Suddenly there was a loud and piercing shriek that reverberated through the whole house, followed by silence.

Conrad Veidt said a shiver of real fear ran down his spine, but after that final outburst the house was so much better that it was no longer difficult to live in. As the days and weeks and months passed, there were fewer and fewer disturbances, and for the first time since they had moved into the house Lily and Conrad Veidt felt there was a peaceful atmosphere.

One of the clergyman who visited the house was clairvoyant, and afterwards he told Conrad Veidt that a woman had been murdered on the stairs and a man had committed suicide in the back bedroom of the house. Although they never succeeded in establishing the truth or otherwise of the matter, the Veidts came across several tales associated with the house, and there were stories of an unhappy couple and either a murder or a suicide pact, but with the atmosphere of the house so much improved the Veidts – and especially Lily Veidt – thought it best to leave things alone.

From time to time strange sounds were still heard, strange things 'happened' and small but inexplicable disturbances still occurred; however, they were so minor and more irritating than really disturbing, and the human forms were seen no more – or at least only once more.

Several weeks after the exhaustive exorcism, when Lily and Conrad Veidt were congratulating themselves that they had done the right thing and that it was virtually the end of the matter, Conrad Veidt had occasion to visit the 'haunted' room one evening. As soon as he entered the room, he knew the ghostly couple were there. The old atmosphere of tension, hatred, unhappiness and frustration filled the icy-cold room. He hurriedly collected the item he had come for and made to leave the room when he saw the couple standing in his way in the open doorway. The man seemed to be glaring at him with ill-concealed hatred, while the woman cowered beside him. Conrad stopped in his tracks. Then he closed his eyes and concentrated, using all his will-power to dispel the forms from his path and from the house. He quickly found he was becoming drained and exhausted by the effort, but when he could no longer continue and he opened his eyes, the ghostly forms had disappeared, and neither he nor his wife ever saw them again.

Years after his death the form of the German-born character actor reportedly returned at a séance in Bishop Auckland through the mediumship of Betty Dawson. The figure of Conrad

Veidt was recognized by Mrs Josephine Jobson, who had worked with the actor at Denham Studios in 1938.

Tom Lethbridge, that unique and quite remarkable 'explorer of the unknown',[2] once told me about a very curious old house in the close of a cathedral town in the West of England where an exorcism was carried out – and he had some definite views on the use of a crucifix in exorcisms, but first his story of the haunted house.

After dinner one night with a friend who was a canon and his nephew, they went over to the haunted house to meet a mutual friend, a schoolmaster. In one room Lethbridge noticed a large crucifix hanging on the wall, and in another room they found the schoolmaster, looking acutely miserable. He said he had just seen the ghost that haunted the house, quite distinctly, on the stairs. Tom Lethbridge and his friend immediately left the schoolmaster and went to see for themselves.

At the foot of the stairs they were confronted by 'a wall of icy cold, a distinctly unpleasant feeling'. The two men looked at each other and stepped on the first tread of the stairs together. The electric light was on and at first they saw nothing unusual, but they noticed that the coldness seemed to retreat before them as they advanced. They took a second step up the stairway, and the coldness retreated again. In this way they were convinced that, step by step, they pushed whatever it was on the stairs up the complete flight, and at the top they felt they had cornered it, for there was only one more step.

They both felt very frightened at this stage and they half expected some revolting horror to materialize and confront them. They linked arms and took the last step together. Instantly they both felt the coldness pass them, and it was behind them, lower down the stairway. They no longer felt any fear, together they believe they hustled it back down the whole stairway but at the bottom it slipped back again behind them and, presumably, continued its vigil of the stairway.

After some discussion it was decided to report the matter to the bishop, and they went over in a body. He said he could do nothing that night but he promised to arrange a proper exorcism the very next day. During the course of conversation they discovered that he was the person who had hung the crucifix in the room at the end of the hall, facing the stairway.

Although he was not present at the exorcism next day, Tom told me it was certainly carried out, with bell, book and candle, in every room in the house, but Tom and his friend were for more active measures and they set about exploring the room with the crucifix. After some difficulties they removed a section of the panelling and discovered a space – but there was no skeleton, no bones, nothing in fact except a few mother-of-pearl counters. There the matter ended as far as Tom Lethbridge was concerned.

Some weeks later a new master, who was in holy orders, moved into the haunted house. Soon after his arrival he related a terrible dream in which he had seen the door of the bathroom, next to his bedroom, open and a horrible hairy figure emerge. As it had approached him, the reverend gentleman had snatched the sheet from his bed and held it up in front of him, although he said afterwards he had felt the form to be a friendly one. When he lowered the sheet, the form had disappeared. When he heard that the house was haunted, the new master carried out his own exorcism, and this, it seems, was too much for the haunting entity, which departed, and the house was thereafter unhaunted.

On the question of the use of a crucifix in such circumstances, Tom Lethbridge felt it would have no effect whatever on a ghost. As he put it, 'You need some active jamming effect to interrupt the transmission.' He had some very original theories about ghosts, and anyone interested should read his fascinating books, especially *Ghost and Ghoul*.

Let us now consider a very different lay exorcism. We have already met Captain Eric Myers, who was a Ghost Club member for some years until his untimely death. He related a personal experience of lay exorcism at a Ghost Club meeting. He said that his intelligence work as an Army captain in West Africa and in Egypt had convinced him that alleged accounts of psychic assault could be explained as the result of a disordered mind, and this he always believed until he encountered an 'enraged devil' at the Buckinghamshire home of some friends.

The subject of the exorcism was a 26-year-old woman who had once been a cheerful and sport-loving person with an excellent career in a bank – until she began experimenting with drugs and drink. She seemed to change very quickly: she gave up her job, and before long she thought of nothing but her addictions; eventually the help of a psychiatrist was sought, and soon she was persuaded to give up the harmful practices she had been following but there was little improvement in her health. She suffered repeated bouts of severe depression and talked of suicide; indeed, she told her parents that the only thing that kept her from taking her own life was the fact that it would mean leaving her pet dog. Then suddenly the dog became mysteriously and violently ill. Its life was saved by a veterinary surgeon, and its owner then admitted that she had given it poison so that it would not grieve over her death ...

Eric Myers and his wife Mollie knew the family, and they arrived for the weekend. At this time the daughter seemed comparatively normal, physically and mentally, although somewhat reserved. However, her parents were still very worried about her, and Eric thought the problem might be helped by the laying-on of hands. It did not occur to him at this time that the girl might be harbouring a demon.

Later in the day he carried out a single laying-on of hands on the daughter, and he felt that this was so beneficial that he decided to repeat the experiment. With hindsight, he told the Ghost Club members, he believed the initial laying-on ceremony had disturbed an evil entity within the young woman and that the entity then made efforts to defend itself.

As the young woman walked towards him for a second session of the laying-on of hands, he saw her face change. Just for a moment Eric Myers saw, or thought he saw, not an ordinary young lady but a hideous and wizened old crone, hunched and scrawny and looking about ninety years old! Her eyes seemed to glow with hatred, and there was a stench like that of rotten vegetation. Then, as suddenly as it had happened, the illusion disappeared and the young woman appeared to be quite normal again. Convinced by this transitory transformation that a demon was occupying the body of the unfortunate woman, Eric Myers decided to attempt an exorcism.

With the full co-operation of everyone concerned, he carried out the exorcism in the kitchen of the house, using words and ritual movements which he had obtained from the Cabbala, the mystic and secret lore, originally Jewish, that contains names of power that have been harnessed and used by occultists in ritual ceremonies for centuries.

To ensure his own protection, Eric Myers called on the four archangels, Gabriel, Michael, Uriel and Raphael, to surround him with strength and to protect him, and then, using words of power and benediction that he had found helpful in the past, he made the sign of the cross and touched the forehead, lower abdomen and right and left shoulders of the woman as he said the words: 'Thou art ... the Kingdom ... the Power ... and the Glory.' Finally in this protective ritual, he turned to face the east, clasped his hands together before his chest and intoned, 'Forever, Amen.'

Captain Eric Myers now faced the subject of his exorcism and addressed the occupying entity: 'Whoever you are and wherever you are from, leave this person and come forth.' When nothing happened, he repeated the command more forcibly. Still nothing happened, and he then accepted that the lay exorcism had not been successful. Sometimes, Myers knew, exorcists are faced with an entity so entrenched that two or more exorcisms are required to remove them, and he thought this must be such a case – until he saw the hag again. Then he realized that he was being deceived by the sly spirit, which had left the woman at the time of his exorcism but was hovering about the house, awaiting its opportunity to reoccupy her body.

Eric Myers said he saw the entity quite distinctly. It was hovering outside the kitchen window, a few feet from the ground, with arms outstretched and pointing in an accusing fashion. It resembled for all the world a gruesome pantomime witch, and its eyes seemed to be fixed on him. Suddenly it launched itself straight at him, coming right through the glass of the closed window and making a horrible screeching sound.

Myers found himself praying aloud for the protection of the archangels, and when the ghastly form was no more than a couple of feet from him, he saw a golden sword materialize in front of him. The hideous entity was impaled on the sword, and it immediately lost all shape and turned into a column of black smoke which diminished into a wisp and then vanished completely. Captain Myers knew then that he had finally vanquished the evil entity.

Myers told Ghost Club members that at one time he would have regarded such a story with considerable scepticism. He had heard accounts of evil manifestations but thought they had little substance or fact, but the sudden appearance of that golden sword had been dramatic and a real answer to prayer. In a moment of terror he had sought protection and had received it. Soon the young woman resumed a normal life and was completely delivered from harmful influences.

Exorcisms of different kinds have been carried out at many well-known haunted houses. At historic Glamis Castle, perhaps the most haunted building in Britain, there have long been stories of exorcisms carried out over the centuries.

Here, with stories of a family monster and half-a-dozen ghosts, a secret room, mysterious sounds and in fact mysteries without number – and murders and suicides said to have taken place within its walls, it is little wonder that, after all else has been tried, exorcisms have been attempted. Sportsman, author and ghost hunter James Wentworth Day (1899–1983) told me that he had seen reports of exorcisms at Glamis carried out by some of the most important ecclesiastics of the various Churches and attended by some of 'the highest in the land'. One exorcism only seemed to make matters worse but a fairly recent one seems to have caused things to become much quieter and less troublesome at atmospheric Glamis.

Once, when I was at beautiful, brooding Glamis, I spent some time in what was regarded as the 'most haunted room', and I could well understand Sir Walter Scott's feelings. During a night he spent there he saw no ghost but said afterwards: 'I must own that when the door was shut I began to consider myself as too far from the living and somewhat too near the dead.'

Details of exorcisms at Glamis are hard to come by, but it does seem that, in spite of many having been carried out there, of all denominations, the castle and its immediate precincts are still occasionally haunted.

Chingle Hall is often spoken of these days as being currently the 'most haunted house in England', and I must say that there is, or was, a lot of good evidence to warrant such a statement, although I have often wondered exactly how you can really decide which house is in fact more haunted than another: by the number of ghosts, by the number of reported incidents, by the variety of phenomena, by the number of witnesses, by the length of the haunting, or what?

Anyway, at Chingle Hall, a fascinatingly hidden house built in the form of a cross, it does seem that ghostly forms have been

seen and heard dozens of times, although I have never actually
seen anything of a paranormal nature there during the score of
times I have visited Chingle over the years. The late owner, Mrs
Margaret Howarth, told my wife and me, unequivocally, 'This
house is undoubtedly haunted ... we hear ghostly footsteps
constantly; once they were heard by eight people. Door latches
move, night after night; doors open by themselves; dogs'
hackles rise; objects move; a cloaked form walks in the garden
and in the Priest Room ...'

Chingle Hall is believed to have been the birthplace of John
Wall (1620–79), a Franciscan priest who was one of the last
English Roman Catholic martyrs, and it is the 'spirit' of John
Wall that many people believe lingers at Chingle to this day.

Exorcisms at Chingle Hall have been carried out by local and
visiting clergymen and always in the Priest Room, undoubtedly
the most haunted room in the house. On several occasions
experienced Ghost Club investigators have heard loud bangs
and thuds originate from the direction of the 'priest hole' and
appear to travel across the floor, up the wall and across the
ceiling![3]

As far as exorcisms at Chingle are concerned, when it had to
be accepted that an Anglican service had no effect, a Roman
Catholic exorcism was conducted with full rites, but still with no
apparent effect, and it was then decided to hold a service of
exorcism which combined Anglican and Roman Catholic clergy
and incorporated the use of a pre-Reformation 'praying-cross',
long preserved at Chingle; but for better or for worse the ghosts
at Chingle still seem to walk.

A curious open-air exorcism was carried out some years ago at
the spot near Clouds Hill, Lawrence of Arabia's cottage near
Bovington in Dorset, where that enigmatic figure met his death
and where, subsequently, the throaty roar of a powerful Brough
Superior motorcycle was reportedly heard on many occasions
although nothing was seen.

Lawrence of Arabia used to love to roar about the countryside
on his beloved Brough Superior, and he met his death on the
machine in somewhat puzzling circumstances. Henry Williamson, to whom Lawrence had sent a telegram of welcome in
answer to a note suggesting he should visit, minutes before his
accident, told me on several occasions that he was convinced
that Lawrence's death was no accident; indeed the coroner at

the inquest said it was 'a most unsatisfactory situation', but perhaps it is appropriate that the man whose whole life was something of a mystery should meet his death in mysterious circumstances, for Williamson was by no means alone in his suspicions. In any case Lawrence's ghost has been seen at Clouds Hill, though not on the stretch of road where the accident occurred, nor is anything seen there, but the sound of that unmistakable machine has been heard racing towards people; then, when the machine is apparently only a short distance away, the noise of the motorcycle ceases abruptly. In the records of the Ghost Club there are a dozen such reports, independent and each person being unaware that other people have heard the same sounds and thinking that they are unique in hearing them.

A local vicar, visiting Clouds Hill, is among the many people who have thought they caught a glimpse of the white-robed figure of Lawrence entering the little cottage that he loved. When the clergyman made his way to the scene of the accident, he told me, he distinctly heard the roar of Lawrence's machine coming towards him. At any moment he expected to see a motorcycle but he saw nothing and then, as inexplicably as it began, the sounds ceased and all was quiet.

This vicar told me he had no worries about Lawrence's haunting the cottage, where he found peace and happiness, but he was perturbed at the ghostly sounds that haunted the fatal spot on the road, which he felt might be a danger to other road-users, and he conducted a kind of exorcism at the place and repeated it seven days running. The first exorcism was carried out on 13 May 1985, fifty years to the day after the fatal accident, and since this series of exorcisms I have not received any further reports of the 'ghostly' sounds.

Another historic house where exorcisms have been conducted with some success is Leith Hall in Aberdeenshire. Here, where American author Elizabeth Byrd lived for five years, ghosts walked and she and her husband experienced a wealth of ghostly activity.

Elizabeth Byrd told me she knew nothing of any ghosts when she moved in, but it was not long before her husband saw the ghost of a Victorian lady in the Leith Bedroom. Elizabeth Byrd repeatedly heard soft footsteps on the third floor, 'sometimes a slow shuffle, at other times a scampering sound such as a child or a puppy might make'; there was also a 'padding noise', almost like a large dog padding about, and one particular door often closed by itself on still and windless nights. And then Elizabeth Byrd awakened one morning to see the ghost of a man with a bandaged head standing beside her bed; he took a step forward towards her and then suddenly vanished.

Subsequently Elizabeth Byrd told me that the ghost she had seen was probably that of Colonel Alexander Sebastian Leith-Hay (1818–1900) or possibly John Leith, the laird of Leith Hall, who was shot in 1763, his widow being convicted of the murder. After a perfect welter of preternatural happenings and experiences by herself, her husband and friends and visitors to the place, she arranged for an exorcism; when this had no effect, she arranged for a further one to be carried out, and thereafter peace seems to have reigned at Leith Hall.

Marelands at Bentley in Hampshire is a typical example of a delightful country family house being haunted and being exorcized. Although the property has been much altered over the years, its various owners and occupants have added character to the house, which was, by all accounts, very haunted at one time.

Christopher Hussey, writing in *Country Life*, described Marelands as 'a house of memories, some charming, some sinister', and I think that is a very fair and true assessment. Once the house belonged to the Stawell family, probably at the end of the eighteenth century, and Lord Stawell's agent, a man named Salisbury, apparently lived there; a man who reportedly '... dropped suddenly out of his chair and was dead in a moment, on the eve of his birthday, while his wife was preparing an elegant entertainment for his friends the day following ...'

Tradition has long associated Lord Stawell with the murder of an illegitimate child, and one story tells of Lord Stawell himself murdering the child he had had by a housekeeper at Marelands and burying the child beneath a hearthstone; another version has it that his agent or steward carried out the dastardly deed in one of the bedrooms – perhaps the bedroom long known as 'the haunted room' on the west side of the house and possessing a most unusual domed ceiling – and a very curious atmosphere. At all events, '... the calcinated bones of a child were found beneath the hearthstone in one of the ground floor rooms in 1918'. (Or did all this happen at Hinton Ampner, another lovely house owned by Lord Stawell where an identical legend pertains?)

My old friend Dorothea St Hill Bourne regaled me with stories of her visits to Marelands long ago when both she and her sister felt there was 'something sinister' about the staircase and they found 'the haunted room' 'most definitely haunted'. One of the Joy family, who have lived at Marelands for many years, used to say that the house was 'very haunted' and 'had a dreadful feeling at times', particularly 'the haunted room'. She firmly believed that this was the room where the murder had taken place, committed by 'the wicked Lord Stawell' and his ghost had haunted the house for years – until in fact a service of exorcism had been held there.

As recently as June 1989 Michael Joy told me that years ago there was indeed an exorcism in the so-called 'haunted room' at Marelands. There have been people who have slept in that domed chamber and refused to spend another night in the house; on the other hand there have been many people who have spent untroubled nights in the same room. One visitor spent 'an awful night' there, absolutely certain that there was someone in the room; he saw nothing but continually switched on the light for most of the night because no sooner had he put it off than he was again convinced that there was someone in the room.

Things apparently became so bad at one period that the then owner arranged for a 'specialist' in exorcism to come over from Winchester and carry out an exorcism with bell, book and candle. She did what she could but claimed she was stopped in the process and was almost choked by 'something'; she said she would have to spend a night in the room and then try again. She did so and eventually completed the exorcism. It seems it was partially if not totally successful; at all events, Marelands is today a charming and peaceful home for a delightful family.

And on that cheerful note let us come to the end of this exploration of the curious rite of exorcism: the casting-out of evil spirits by the use of prayer or a holy name or some unconventional means. It would be comforting to accept the premise, but in some fifty years study of the subject I have yet to encounter an 'evil' ghost. But perhaps I am trespassing into the final chapter, which must look, as objectively as possible, at all the evidence for this curious but enduring rite.

9   Some Final Thoughts on Exorcism

It is clear to me that exorcism is not a cut-and-dried rite that either is or is not effective in its purpose. The generally accepted idea of exorcism is that a power of good is paramount over a power of evil. After this somewhat exhaustive and wide investigation I still find the idea of exorcism, as it is usually understood and in circumstances in which it is usually carried out, difficult to accept, since all the evidence I have collected over the past fifty years does not suggest to me that there is anything evil about ghosts – which may be why exorcism so often appears to be ineffective.

In any case, how do we explain those incidents where the object of the exorcism is a material object – how can that be evil? The strange story told about the sounds of Lawrence of Arabia's motorcycle being exorcized immediately springs to mind, which I have related in the previous chapter. How can prayers and incantations have any effect on a sound? And yet they seem to have done so. Even if it is postulated that the sound is evil in origin (although I don't see why it should be), surely the exorcism should be addressed to the evil concocting the sound, not the sound itself.

In similar vein I personally find it difficult to accept that prayers, holy water and incantations can have any real effect against 'thought forms' or 'atmospheric photographs', which many ghosts seem to be; or for that matter against cyclic (regularly occurring) ghosts which apparently require 365 days to build up sufficient 'power' to manifest; or 'crisis apparitions', 'time slips' or even 'poltergeists' that seem to draw energy from human beings or from the atmosphere and throw objects about but *without evil* intent, I would submit.

Of course there are haunted houses where exorcism might well be tried, and I am reminded of the house close to

Fordingbridge in Hampshire, a house that was the scene of one of the most horrific crimes in recent years, and a house that is due for demolition because the new owners are unable to face living within walls that had witnessed such evil – and they may well be doing the wise thing.

The Anglican Rev. Christopher Neil-Smith, who may have personally performed over 3,000 exorcisms, says that evil should be treated as an actual force rather than an abstract idea; he says that merely performing the ritual of exorcism is not enough; the exorcisms of Jesus were 'of the Holy Spirit', and the priest conducting an exorcism has to be guided by the Holy Spirit, and he therefore emphasizes the need for prayer, spiritual awareness and dedication to the service of others as absolutely essential for exorcists.

That I can understand, for psychiatrists have realized the potential benefit from what appears to be a healing force that can be generated by kindness, higher consciousness and wisdom. I have talked with the psychiatrist Dr R.K. McAll, who has found exorcism effective not only in treating haunted people but also in certain cases of epilepsy and schizophrenia and other forms of mental illness, and cases of alcoholism and drug-addiction. Interestingly enough, the co-operation of the patient is not necessary to the success of the treatment, and in one case a service of exorcism was held in a room near a padded cell where the occupant and subject of the exorcism suddenly quietened down at the crucial point of the ritual and eventually recovered from his mental illness. It may be that the great value of exorcism is that it offers a method of treatment within the context of a religious framework, and Dr McAll is prominent among those who have seemingly excelled in this particular work. Most religious exorcists consider themselves to be fulfilling the Lord's command to 'preach the Gospel, heal the sick and cast out demons'.

There is also the down-to-earth, no-nonsense 'exorcist' who seems equally successful on occasion. I remember when the diviner Robert Leftwich visited us on one occasion he told me that when he and his family first occupied their delightful home in Sussex, built on the site of an earlier, sixteenth-century house, they began to hear stories of a ghostly 'lady in white' who was reputed to walk down the garden periodically. Although they met a number of people who maintained that they had actually seen the ghost, the new occupants were not too concerned about the matter.

However, after a while, odd things began to happen inside the house. Mrs Leftwich would suddenly be aware that a hand was resting on one of her shoulders while she was working alone in the kitchen, perhaps at the sink or attending to something in the oven, and many times, when their two boys were much younger, both Robert and his wife would hear noisy disturbances from the upper part of their home. Thinking that the boys were up to some games, Robert would set off upstairs to investigate, but halfway up the stairs the noises always ceased, and when Robert entered the boys' bedroom, they were invariably found to be fast asleep. Other disturbances included the distinct impression that something or somebody passed by Robert's open study door; there were innumerable instances when a peculiar aroma resembling rotten fish pervaded the kitchen, always followed by the presence of a cold vertical column of air that defied all normal physical laws by not being instantly dispersed by the surrounding warm air or the movement of objects.

One evening, Robert believed he located the exact position of the haunting entity in the kitchen with the help of his divining-rods, and he put his rods to one side and boldly addressed the 'ghost'. He said that, while 'it' obviously had an older and possibly greater right to be there than he and his family, the house had now become their home, and some of the present occupants and especially the children could not understand such activity, and therefore if any future manifestations could be restricted to non-materialistic activity, it would be greatly appreciated.

In addition, and to prove to his satisfaction that 'it' had understood his request, Robert suggested that the entity should move a large oil painting that hung above the fireplace in the sitting-room during the night and he would accept any change of position the following morning as an indication that all would be well in the future.

Next morning the elder son of the family was first up and he came running into his parents' bedroom exclaiming that burglars must have broken in during the night, for the sitting-room was in a terrible mess; he also mentioned that the large oil painting had been removed from its position over the fireplace and was on the floor on the other side of the room. Investigation proved that a considerable disturbance had indeed taken place in the sitting-room, and in addition to the movement of the oil painting a number of delicate porcelain ornaments had been removed from their places on the mantelpiece and lay broken on the floor.

After that incident the Leftwich family were only very occasionally aware of an intangible force in the house, and they were certainly never again bothered to any serious degree.

Another example of what might be termed the unorthodox approach has been used by the cleric and author Jack Richardson, who has revealed that he has carried out the occasional exorcism – including one in his own vicarage! Someone he knew 'came back as a ghost', and although his former colleagues were quite happy at his appearing in their midst from time to time, 'he' did tend to be something of a nuisance at times, so one day Jack Richardson took the matter in hand. He simply said, in his quiet way: 'We enjoyed your company in life; and we do like your visits now and again but you *are* overdoing it a bit, you know. Why don't you move on, old boy, and leave us alone ...' Apparently there were no more visitations!

The Rev. Dominic Walker, whom we have already met, revealed in an interview in 1988 that he had personally investigated more than a thousand cases of paranormal activity. I believe he is on the right lines when he says that many cases of so-called 'possession' are nothing to do with spirits or the spirit world but are simply '... due to the state of mind of the person concerned and psychological counselling can often stop the "phenomena".'

Among his adventures in haunted houses Dominic Walker revealed that he had once been struck in the back by a large jar of coffee that had stood on a shelf several feet away: 'It just shot off the shelf, as if thrown by some unseen hand, and hit me before I could react and it left quite a bruise ...' I wonder whether the evocative phrase 'as if thrown by an unseen hand' is really that of Dominic Walker; and if he was hit in the back, presumably the object came from behind him, since he had no time to react – how then can he state categorically, 'it just shot off the shelf', when he did not see it begin movement. I would need to know a lot more about this incident, the people who

were present and their precise positions at the time, before I
could accept this particular incident as a 'poltergeist
phenomenon', not least because most poltergeist-projected
objects, when they strike a person, do not appear to have any
force, and it is almost like a feather striking a person.

In the 1988 interview Dominic Walker revealed that he was
once called to help a young woman who had become involved
with Satanists, and she did seem to be possessed by some
strange force. 'The woman writhed, screamed and swore until
she became so strong we needed two men to hold her down,'
and then she '... gabbled away in Norwegian, a language she
had no knowledge of in her normal state'. In fact, the interview
stated, she spoke in the voices of three different men.

The woman became violent during the actual exorcism
ceremony and blasphemed on seeing the priest's crucifix.
'When I sprinkled her with holy water, ugly red patches
developed where it had touched her skin,' the exorcist is quoted
as stating. That I would have liked to have seen, and again I
would welcome confirmatory evidence from medical men who,
presumably, were present. After half an hour the woman is
stated to have become calm and '... was quite normal after she
recovered consciousness'; I for one had not been aware that she
had been 'unconscious'.

When he visited a haunted house in South London, Dominic
Walker was given a portrait of the ghost haunting the house! A
woman relative of the afflicted family was an artist, and when
the figure appeared in the bedroom she was occupying, she
promptly drew what she saw – and neighbours immediately
recognized the face as that of a former occupant who had
committed suicide in the house. The Rev. Dominic Walker is
stated in the published interview to have decided to bless the
picture of the ghost, and as he said the words 'Holy, holy, holy',
'... the ghost appeared to smile and then simply faded away and
it has not been seen since'.

When I was researching my *Ghosts of North West England*, I
talked with Sir Walter Bromley-Davenport, whose stately home,
Capesthorne Hall in Cheshire, has long been troubled by ghosts.
Sir Walter, a former Grenadier Guards boxing champion, told
Ghost Clubber Dr George Owen, 'One night I saw a line of
shadowy, spectre-like figures descending the steps into the
family vault in my private chapel' and another time he saw a

grey form gliding along a corridor. Other members of the family and visitors have reported a variety of ghosts and ghostly happenings over the years at Capesthorne Hall.

Sir Walter told me in 1977: 'Where the ghosts appear we have the spot blessed by the church.' It does not seem to have resolved the problem. Quite recently Sir Walter Bromley-Davenport called on his chaplain, Canon Archibald Sholto Douglas, to bless the property again and help the ghost or ghosts at the same time. 'I'm not taking any chances,' Sir Walter said at the time. 'I am asking the Almighty to help this poor spirit. It may be it wants to move on to another life in the next world ... of course it may not want to. Then I shall just have to put up with it ...'

Clues to the possible origin of some exorcism customs are to be found in ancient rituals that combat the Evil Eye – the eye that brings misfortune. Much-travelled author Nina Epton once told me about her encounters with the Evil Eye in Morocco some thirty years ago.

She was told of a sculptor, Tomás, who was astonished one day when one of his models brought him a snail, entreating him to wear it round his neck. 'You have such a good face,' she told him. 'Somebody is bound to be jealous and cast the Evil Eye on you ... the snail will protect you.'

A Moroccan standing nearby pricked up his ears at the mention of the Evil Eye and said, 'You may laugh if you like, but it cannot be denied that the Evil Eye exists and that it can be effective. I used to scoff at such tales until I witnessed a very strange incident when I was in my teens ...'

The gist of the story is that his mother had bought a new luxury sewing-machine of which she was very proud, a machine that soon became the envy of many of the women in the immediate neighbourhood. Within a few days the machine suddenly stopped and refused to function. No one could discover what was wrong, and in the end an engineer from the shop where the machine had been purchased visited the house. He was just as puzzled as everyone else and could not find anything wrong with the machine, although he took it to pieces and put it back together again. In the end he had to admit defeat and left, saying he would contact the headquarters of the firm that had manufactured the machine.

When he had gone, an old servant, Fatima, suggested that someone had cast the Evil Eye over the machine. She said she knew a lot about such things and she had a pretty shrewd idea as to who the culprit might be. She was given a free hand to see what she could do in the matter, and Nina Epton's informant decided to watch the servant closely.

Fatima dressed to go out, donning her voluminous *jell-aba* and a veil. The fact that she put on a veil was a little surprising, for she did not need to do so at her age, and in fact she did not do so as a rule. She then hid a little shovel and a bag beneath her *jell-aba* and walked quickly away, followed stealthily by the young son of the house.

Fatima hurried to the home of one of his mother's friends, a rather gushing type of woman, and there she hid, watching the house. After about half-an-hour both watchers were rewarded by hearing a familiar, high-pitched woman's voice coming down the street. It was the friend returning home, accompanied by her sister. As soon as they had entered the house, Fatima appeared, shovel in hand, and began to scrape the dust of the footprints of the gushing friend into the little bag she had brought for the purpose; it might have been gold for the care she took of it.

Back home the young man was confronted by Fatima, who had spotted him following her, and she told him not to breathe a word to his mother of what she had done and where she had been or the counter-spell would not work. Fatima then went to her mistress, still sitting puzzled in front of the non-working machine. Fatima walked up to her, drew out the little bag and, throwing the contents over the machine, began to murmur weird incantations of which neither the mother nor her son could understand a word. Fatima was immediately upbraided for throwing filth over the new machine but she was unrepentant and merely said, 'Now see whether the machine works ...' Her mistress tried the machine, as she had a hundred times before, but this time it worked and went on working as smoothly as ever, and they had no more trouble with it.

Finally, in this summing-up of exorcism and what it means, when really all one can do is give examples of exorcisms that have appeared to be affective, it is interesting to note that the Rev. John Richards of Queen's College, Birmingham, takes a rather different view from that of many of his fellow clergy. He does not believe the Christian Church has any 'counter-magic' against the forces of evil, and those who resort to exorcism should do so, he feels, only as part of the Christian ministry of healing. 'The alleged issue of crucifixes to police when searching for maniacs known to be invovled in magic or the use of holy water in blessing places should not be used,' he maintains; 'except when they are an expression of the prayers of the Church.'

John Richards regards Christian exorcism not as a fight to the death between the power of good and those of evil but rather as 'a demonstration of the power and love of the Lordship of Christ over His world'; in common with many clergymen he prefers the use of such words as 'dispossession', 'redemption' and 'liberation' to the emotive word 'exorcism'. He accepts that there are some gifted priests who have had a lot of experience in dealing with evil forces in people and who can recognize the character of mental and psychic illness, but he believes that one of the most powerful of all 'exorcisms' is in fact used every day by millions of people, when they pray: 'Deliver us from evil'.

I always had a lot of time for Dom Robert Petitpierre OSB as an exorcist; he seemed to me to keep his feet firmly on the ground most of the time and in most cases that he was involved in, and he had refreshing honesty in viewing these difficult and involved matters. In one of his last letters to me, when I had mentioned the increasing number of people who seemed to think they were possessed of evil spirits, he wrote: 'As you know most of the people who ring up in a panic are more of mentally disturbed types than of folk attacked by evil spirits. When someone says they are "possessed" it is usually not true, as no little devil would let on!'

My summing-up has to be: Exorcism sometimes works for some people. A poor result for an exhaustive and comprehensive exploration? Not really, for if it *really does work* sometimes, isn't that in its way some sort of miracle? And one fact is, I think, patently clear: a simple exorcism with no religious connotations whatever is just as likely to be successful as a full-blown religious ceremony and ritual. Now there *is* food for thought!

Notes

1   Exorcism: Ancient and Modern
1. As given in Augustine's *City of God*, Book XXII, chapter 8

4   Exorcism and Possession
1. As stated in my *Dictionary of the Supernatural* (Harrap, 1978)
2. Ainslie Meares, *Strange Places and Simple Truths* (Souvenir Press, 1969)
3. Marianne Sinclair, *Hollywood Lolita* (Plexus, 1988)

5   Exorcism and Witchcraft
1. Beati, Richalm, etc., *Liber Revelationum De Insidiis et Versutiis Daemonum adversus Homines*
2. Beati, Richalm, etc., op. cit.

6   Exorcism and Vampires
1. The Hon. Ralph Shirley: educated at Winchester and New College, Oxford; director of Rider, the publisher, and founder of *Occult Review*
2. *Modern Greek Folklore and Ancient Greek Folklore* (Cambridge University Press, 1910)
3. See my introduction to *Thirteen Famous Ghost Stories* (Dent's Everyman's Library, 1977)
4. This book has long been out of print, in both hardback and paperback

8   More Exorcisms in Haunted Houses, etc.
1. Father Cyril Martindale once addressed the Society for Psychical Research on the subject of 'The Apparitions at Fatima'.

2. As noted in my book *The Ghost Hunters* (Robert Hale, 1985)
3. The facts of this very curious case are detailed in my volume entitled *This Haunted Isle* (Harrap, 1984)

Select Bibliography

Alexander, Marc, *The Devil Hunter* (Sphere, 1981)

Andrews, William, *Legal Lore* (William Andrews, 1897)

Augustine, Saint, *The City of God* (Dent, 1945 revision)

Bailey, J.C., *Rogan* (Arcturus Press, 1988)

Baker, Roger, *Binding the Devil* (Sheldon Press 1974)

Baroja, Julio Caro, *The World of the Witches* (Weidenfeld & Nicolson, 1964)

Beza, Marcu, *Paganism in Roumanian Folklore* (Dent, 1928)

Branden, Victoria, *Understanding Ghosts* (Gollancz, 1980)

Brown, Raymond Lamont, *Phantoms of the Theatre* (Satellite Books, 1978)

Buckhardt, V.R., *Chinese Customs* (South China Morning Post, 1958)

Budge, E.A. Wallis, *Literature of the Ancient Egyptians* (Dent, 1914)

Burton, Jean, *Heyday of a Wizard* (Harrap, 1948)

Cannon, Alexander, *Powers That Be* (Dutton, New York, 1935)

Coulton, G.B., *Five Centuries of Religion* (Cambridge University Press, 1923)

Cristiani, L., *Satan and the Modern World* (Skeffington, 1959)

Dearing, Trevor, *Exit the Devil* (Logos Publishing, 1976)

Eadie, John, *Biblical Cyclopaedia* (Richard Griffin, 1855)

Epton, Nina, *Saints and Sorcerers* (Cassell, 1958)

Flammarion, Camille, *Haunted Houses* (Fisher Unwin, 1924)

Forster, John, *Life of Charles Dickens* (Dent, 1927 Edition)

Gifford, Edward S., *The Evil Eye* (Macmillan, New York, 1958)

Givry, Grillot de, *Witchcraft, Magic and Alchemy* (University Books, New York, 1931)

Goodman, Felicitas D., *How About Demons* (Indiana University Press, 1988)

Hart, Roger, *Witchcraft* (Wayland, 1971)

Haynes, Renée, *The Society for Psychical Research – A History* (Macdonald, 1982)

Henning, A.C., *Haunted Borley* (private pub., 1949)

Hill, Douglas and Pat Williams, *The Supernatural* (Aldus Books, 1965)

Hoppé, A.J., *Readers Guide to Everyman's Library* (Dent, 1960)

Huxley, Aldous, *The Devils of Loudun* (Chatto & Windus, 1952)

Johns, June, *King of the Witches* (Peter Davies, 1969)

Jones, William, *Credulities, Past and Present* (Chatto & Windus, 1880)

Langton, Edward, *Supernatural* (Rider, 1934)

———, *Satan: A Portrait* (Skeffington, 1945)

Lea, H.C., *The Inquisition of the Middle Ages* (Harper, New York, 1888)

Leslie, Shane, *Shane Leslie's Ghost Book* (Hollis & Carter, 1955)

Lethbridge, T.C., *Ghost and Ghoul* (Routledge & Kegan Paul, 1961)

Lockhart, J.G., *Curses, Lucks and Talismans* (Geoffrey Bles, 1938)

Maple, Eric, *The Dark World of Witches* (Robert Hale, 1962)

———, *The Domain of Devils* (Robert Hale, 1966)

———, *The Realm of Ghosts* (Robert Hale, 1964)

McAll, Dr Kenneth, *Healing the Haunted* (Darley Anderson, 1989)

Petitpierre, Dom Robert, *Exorcising Devils* (Robert Hale, 1976)

Picknett, Lynn, *Flights of Fancy* (Ward Lock, 1987)

Pouwels, Louis and Bergier, Jacques, *The Dawn of Magic* (Gibbs & Phillips, 1963)

Price, Harry, *The End of Borley Rectory* (Harrap, 1946)

———, *Poltergeist Over England* (Country Life, 1945)

Richards, John, *But Deliver Us from Evil* (Darton, Longman & Todd, 1974)

Seligmann, Kurt, *Magic, Supernaturalism and Religion* (Allen Lane, 1948)

Shepard, Leslie, *How to Protect Yourself against Black Magic and Witchcraft* (Citadel Press, New Jersey, 1978)

Sinclair, Marianne, *Hollywood Lolita* (Plexus, 1988)

Summers, Montague, *Malleus Maleficarum* (Pushkin Press, edited 1948)

———, *The Vampire in Europe* (Kegan Paul, 1929)

———, *The Werewolf* (Kegan Paul, 1933)

———, *Witchcraft and Black Magic* (Rider, 1945)

Thurston, Herbert, *Ghosts and Poltergeists* (Burns, Oates, 1953)

Uhler, Alfred M., *Cast Out Your Devils* (World's Work, 1939)
Underwood, Peter, *A Host of Hauntings* (Leslie Frewin, 1973)
———, *Deeper Into the Occult* (Harrap, 1975)
———, *Dictionary of the Supernatural* (Harrap, 1978)
———, *Gazetteer of Scottish and Irish Ghosts* (Souvenir Press, 1973)
———, with Dr Paul Tabori, *The Ghosts of Borley* (David & Charles, 1973)
———, *Ghosts of North West England* (Collins, 1978)
———, *Ghosts of Dorset* (Bossiney Books, 1988)
———, *Hauntings* (Dent, 1977)
———, *Boris Karloff – Horror Man* (Leslie Frewin, 1972)
———, *No Common Task – the Autobiography of a Ghost Hunter* (Harrap, 1983)
———, *Thirteen Famous Ghost Stories* (Dent, 1977)
———, *This Haunted Isle* (Harrap, 1984)
———, *The Vampire's Bedside Companion* (Leslie Frewin, 1975)
Watkins, Leslie, *The Real Exorcists* (Methuen, 1983)
Wellesley, Gordon, *Sex and the Occult* (Souvenir Press, 1973)
Wilson, Colin, with Damon Wilson, *The Encyclopaedia of Unsolved Mysteries* (Harrap, 1987)
Wright, Dudley, *Vampires and Vampirism* (Rider, 1924)

Index

Index